366 readings from
CHRISTIANITY

Also in the Global Spirit Library

366 readings from Islam

366 readings from Buddhism

366 readings from Taoism and Confucianism

366 readings from Hinduism

366 readings from Judaism

THE GLOBAL SPIRIT LIBRARY

366 readings from
CHRISTIANITY

edited by

ROBERT VAN DE WEYER

THE PILGRIM PRESS
CLEVELAND, OHIO

ARTHUR JAMES
NEW ALRESFORD, UK

First published in USA and Canada by
The Pilgrim Press,
700 Prospect Avenue East, Cleveland, Ohio 44115

First published in English outside North America by
Arthur James Ltd,
46a West Street, New Alresford, UK, SO24 9AU

Typeset in Monotype Joanna by
Strathmore Publishing Services, London N7

Printed by
Tien Wah Press, Singapore

CONTENTS

SERIES INTRODUCTION

The Global Spirit Library is the first comprehensive collection of the spiritual literature of the world, presented in accessible form. It is aimed at people who belong to a particular religious community, and wish to broaden their spiritual outlook; and at the much larger group, perhaps the majority of people in the world today, who have little or no attachment to a religious community, but seek spiritual wisdom. Each book contains the major writings of one of the world's spiritual traditions.

Much of the world's spiritual literature was designed to be read or heard in small portions, allowing ample time for personal reflection. Following this custom, the books in The Global Spirit Library each consist of an annual cycle of daily readings. Two or more books may be read in parallel at different times of the day; or an entire book may be read straight through. Again following a time-honoured practice, many of the original texts have been condensed.

Spiritual traditions differ from one another in their theological formulations; and the history of humankind is blighted by rivalry between different religious communities. Yet theology is no more than human speculation about truths that are beyond the grasp of the human mind. The writings in these books amply demonstrate that, as men and women actually experience these truths within themselves and others, divisions and rivalries fade, and unity is found. May the third millennium be an era of spiritual unity across the globe.

INTRODUCTION

Christianity is the religion followed by the disciples of Jesus Christ. His disciples were originally given the name 'Christian' in Antioch, possibly by opponents, a few years after the death of Jesus; and they then adopted it with pride.

The common era, known by the initials CE, starts in the year when Jesus was traditionally thought to have been born – although it now seems probable he was born a few years before that date. He was a devout Jew, and in his boyhood studied the Jewish scriptures. Around 30 CE he became a wandering preacher in the region of Galilee in Palestine, where he had grown up. He soon attracted large audiences, and also became famous for the healings and other miracles which he performed. The Jewish authorities turned against him; and with the connivance of the Roman governor he was crucified as a criminal in Jerusalem. Soon after his death his close followers became convinced that he had come back to life. Within a few decades Christianity was spreading across the Roman empire; and by the middle of the first millennium it was the dominant religion of Europe and the Middle East, with outposts deep in Asia.

THE GOSPEL OF JESUS

Shortly after the death of Jesus Christ, in about 33 CE, lists of his sayings were probably circulating amongst Christians. These were followed by several accounts of his life, death and rising from death. Eventually four of the accounts were deemed to be authoritative – those by Matthew, Mark, Luke and John. They became known as 'gospels', meaning that they conveyed good news. The first three gospels have a large amount of common material, and appear to include his authentic sayings; the fourth gospel offers more theological reflection on the story. Christians in practice have not greatly distinguished between one gospel and another, and in their minds have derived a common narrative by taking parts from them all.

The Word

In the beginning was the Word. The Word was with God, and the Word was God. He was with God at the beginning. All things were made through him, and nothing was made except through him. In him was life, and that life was the light of all people. The light shines in the darkness, and the darkness has never overcome it.

A man came, sent by God, whose name was John. He came as a witness to testify to the light, that through him all might believe. He was not the light, but came to bear witness to the light. The true light that enlightens every person was coming into the world.

He was in the world; but the world, though it was made through him, did not recognize him. He came to his own home, and his own people did not accept him. But to all who accepted him, to those who put their trust in him, he gave power to become children of God – born not of human stock, by the physical desire of a human father, but of God. So the Word became flesh; he lived among us, full of grace and truth, and we saw his glory, such glory as befits the Father's only Son.

John 1. 1–14

Announcement of the birth of John

In the reign of Herod, king of Judaea, there was a priest named Zechariah, who belonged to the order of Abijah. His wife, called Elizabeth, was also of priestly descent. Both of them were upright and devout, blamelessly observing all the laws and commands of the Lord. But they had no children, because Elizabeth was barren and both were old.

Once, when his priestly order was on duty and he was serving in the temple, Zechariah was chosen by lot, according to the priestly custom, to burn incense on the altar. So he entered the sanctuary at the hour when the people were gathered outside for prayer. An angel of the Lord appeared to him, standing on the right of the altar where the incense was burnt. When Zechariah saw the angel, he was startled and overcome with fear. But the angel said to him: 'Do not be afraid, Zechariah. God has heard your prayer, and your wife Elizabeth will bear you a son. You will name him John. He will fill you with joy and delight, and many will rejoice at his birth. He will be great in the sight of the Lord. He must drink no wine or strong drink. From his birth he will be filled with the Holy Spirit, and he will bring many of the people of Israel back to the Lord their God. He will go ahead of the Lord, strong and mighty like the prophet Elijah, to reconcile father and child, and to convert the rebellious to the ways of the righteous – to make a people fit for the Lord.'

Luke 1.5–17

Zechariah's doubt

Zechariah said to the angel: 'How can I be sure of this? I am an old man and my wife too is old.' The angel replied: 'I am Gabriel. I stand in the presence of God; and he has sent me to speak to you, and bring you this good news. But, since you did not believe my words, you will lose all power of speech and remain silent until the day when these things take place. At its proper time my promise to you will come true.'

Meanwhile the people were waiting for Zechariah, and wondering why he was spending so long in the sanctuary. When he came out, he could not speak to them, and they realized that he had seen a vision. Unable to say a word, he made signs to them with his hands.

When his period of duty in the temple was over, Zechariah returned home. Some time later his wife Elizabeth conceived, and for five months she did not leave the house. She said to herself: 'The Lord has done this for me. He has looked on me with favour, and taken away my public disgrace.'

Luke 1.18−25

Announcement of the birth of Jesus

In the sixth month of Elizabeth's pregnancy God sent the angel Gabriel to a town in Galilee called Nazareth. The angel had a message for a girl promised in marriage to a man named Joseph, a descendent of David; the girl's name was Mary. The angel came to Mary, and said: 'Peace be with you. The Lord is with you, and has greatly blessed you.'

Mary was deeply troubled by the angel's words, and wondered what they meant. The angel said: 'Do not be afraid, Mary; God has been gracious to you. You will conceive and give birth to a son, and you will name him Jesus. He will be great, and be called the Son of the Most High. The Lord God will give him the throne of his ancestor David, and he will be king over Israel for ever; his reign will never end.'

Mary asked: 'How can this be, since I am still a virgin?' The angel answered: 'The Holy Spirit will come upon you, and the power of the Most High will overshadow you. For this reason the holy child will be called the Son of God. Remember your relative Elizabeth: she was said to be barren, and is very old, but now is six months pregnant. God's promises can never fail.'

Mary said: 'I am the Lord's servant; let it be as you have said.' Then the angel left her.

Luke 1.26–38

Mary's praise

Soon afterwards Mary set out, and hurried to a town in the uplands of Judah. She went to Zechariah's house and greeted Elizabeth. When Elizabeth heard Mary's greeting, the baby stirred in her womb. Elizabeth was filled with the Holy Spirit, and exclaimed: 'God's blessing is on you above all women, and on the child you will bear! Why should I be honoured with a visit from the mother of my Lord? As soon as I heard your greeting, the child in my womb leapt for joy. Blessed is she who believes that the Lord's promise to her will be fulfilled!'

Mary said: 'My soul proclaims the greatness of the Lord, my spirit rejoices in God my saviour; for he has remembered me, his lowly servant. From this day all generations will count me blessed, for the Almighty has done great things for me; his name is holy. He shows mercy to those who honour him, from one generation to another. He has stretched out his mighty arm, and scattered the proud and all their schemes. He has brought down monarchs from their thrones, and lifted up the lowly. He has filled the hungry with good things, and sent the rich away empty. He has kept the promise he made to our ancestors, and come to the help of his servant Israel. He has remembered to show mercy to Abraham and to his descendants for ever.'

Mary stayed about three months with Elizabeth, and then returned home.

Luke 1.39–56

The birth of John

When it was time for Elizabeth to have her child, she gave birth to a son. When the baby was a week old, he was circumcised. The relatives assumed he would be named Zechariah after his father. But his mother spoke up: 'No, his name will be John.' They said to her: 'There is nobody in your family with that name.' Then they made signs to his father, to find out what name he would like the boy to have. Zechariah asked for a writing tablet, and to everyone's astonishment he wrote: 'His name is John.' Immediately his lips and tongue were freed, and he began to speak, praising God.

Zechariah was filled with the Holy Spirit, and spoke this prophecy: 'Blessed be the Lord, the God of Israel. He has come to his people and set them free; he has raised up for us a mighty saviour, a descendent of his servant David. He proclaimed through his prophets long ago that he would save us from our enemies, from the hands of all that hate us. He promised to show mercy to our ancestors, and so remember his holy covenant. He swore an oath to our father Abraham, that he would rescue us from our enemies. He would set us free to serve him without fear, that we might be holy and righteous in his sight all the days of our life. You, my child, will be called a prophet of the Most High. You will go ahead of the Lord to prepare his way, telling his people that they will be saved by the forgiveness of all their sins. In the tender compassion of our God the bright sun of salvation will rise upon us, shining from heaven on all who live in the shadow of death, to guide our steps in the way of peace.'

Luke 1.57, 59–64, 67–79

Joseph's dream

This is how Jesus Christ came to be born. His mother Mary was engaged to Joseph; but before their marriage she found that she was going to have a child by the Holy Spirit. Joseph, being an upright man and wanting to spare her disgrace, decided to break the engagement privately. But an angel of the Lord appeared to him in a dream, and said: 'Joseph, descendant of David, do not be afraid to take Mary home as your wife, because it is by the Holy Spirit that she has conceived. She will bear a son, and you will name him Jesus, for he will save his people from their sins.'

When he awoke, Joseph took Mary home to be his wife, as the angel had directed him; but he did not have intercourse with her until she gave birth to her son. And Joseph named the child Jesus.

Matthew 1.18–21, 24–25

The birth of Jesus

At this time Caesar Augustus ordered that a census be made of the whole Roman Empire. This was the first census, and took place when Quirinius was governor of Syria. People went to their home towns to be registered. Joseph set out from the town of Nazareth in Galilee, to Bethlehem in Judaea; this was the birthplace of David, and Joseph was a descendent of David. His purpose was to register with Mary, who was promised in marriage to him. Mary was pregnant, and while they were in Bethlehem, the time came for her to have her baby. She gave birth to a son, her first-born. She wrapped him in swaddling clothes, and laid him in a manger, because there was no room for them at the inn.

Luke 2. 1—7

The shepherds

In the countryside near to Bethlehem there were shepherds out in the fields, keeping watch through the night over their flock. An angel of the Lord appeared to them, and the glory of the Lord shone round them. They were terrified, but the angel said: 'Do not be afraid. I come to you with good news, which will bring great joy to all people. Today in the town of David your saviour has been born, Christ the Lord. This is a sign for you: you will find a baby wrapped in swaddling clothes, lying in a manger.'

Suddenly with the angel a great company of heaven's angels appeared, singing praise to God: 'Glory to God in the highest heaven, and on earth peace to all in whom he delights.'

When the angels had left them and returned to heaven, the shepherds said to one another: 'Let us go to Bethlehem, and see this event which the Lord has made known to us.' They hurried off and found Mary and Joseph, and the baby lying in a manger. When they saw the child, they related what they had been told about him; and all who heard it were astonished at what the shepherds said. Mary treasured all these things, and pondered them in her heart. The shepherds went back, singing praises to God for all they had heard and seen, just as the angel had told them.

Luke 2.8–20

The wise men

Jesus was born during the reign of King Herod. After his birth wise men from the east arrived in Jerusalem, asking: 'Where is the baby born to be king of the Jews? We saw the rising of his star, and we have come to pay him homage.' King Herod was greatly troubled when he heard this, and so was the whole of Jerusalem. He called together all the chief priests and the teachers of the people, and asked them where the Christ was to be born. 'At Bethlehem in Judaea,' they replied.

Herod summoned the wise men to see him privately, and asked them the exact time the star had appeared. Then he sent them to Bethlehem, saying, 'Go and make a careful search for the child; and when you have found him, bring me word, so that I too may go and pay him homage.'

After listening to the king, the wise men set out, and the star they had seen rising appeared before them. They were overjoyed at the sight of it. The star went ahead of them, and halted above the place where the child lay. They entered the house; and seeing the child with Mary his mother, they fell to their knees in homage. Then they opened their treasure chests, and presented to him gifts of gold, frankincense and myrrh.

But they were warned in a dream not to go back to Herod, so they returned to their own country by a different route.

Matthew 2. 1–5a, 7–12

Flight into Egypt

After the wise men had gone, an angel of the Lord appeared to Joseph in a dream, and said: 'Get up, take the child and his mother, and escape with them to Egypt, and stay there until I tell you. Herod intends to search for the child and kill him.' So Joseph rose up and, taking the child and his mother with him, left that night for Egypt, where he stayed until Herod's death.

When Herod realized that the wise men had tricked him, he flew into a rage. He gave orders that all the boys aged two years or under in Bethlehem and its neighbourhood be killed. This was in accordance with what he had learnt from the wise men about the time when the star had appeared.

After Herod's death an angel of the Lord appeared in a dream to Joseph in Egypt, and said: 'Get up, take the child and his mother, and go back to the land of Israel, for those who wanted to kill the child are dead.' So he rose up and, taking the child and his mother with him, returned to the land of Israel. But when he heard that Archelaus had succeeded his father Herod as king of Judaea, he was afraid to go there. Receiving more instructions in a dream, he went to the region of Galilee, and settled in a town called Nazareth.

Matthew 2.13–15a, 16, 19–23a

Presentation of Jesus in the temple

When the time came for the baby to be circumcised, he was named Jesus, the name given by the angel before he was conceived. Then, after their purification had been completed in accordance with the law of Moses, Joseph and Mary took the child to Jerusalem to present him to the Lord.

At that time a man called Simeon lived in Jerusalem. He was upright and devout, and was waiting for Israel to be saved. The Holy Spirit was upon him, and had assured him that he would not die until he had seen the Christ promised by the Lord. Guided by the Spirit, Simeon came into the temple; and when the parents brought in the child, to do for him what the law required, Simeon took the child in his arms, and praised God: 'Lord, now let your servant depart in peace. Your promise has been fulfilled. With my own eyes I have seen your salvation, which you have prepared in the presence of all peoples: a light to reveal you to the Gentiles, and bring glory to your people Israel.'

Luke 2.21–22, 25–32

Prophecies of Simeon and Anna

The child's father and mother were full of wonder at the things Simeon said about him. Simeon blessed them, and said to Mary his mother: 'The child is destined by God to be a sign that is rejected; and sorrow, like a sharp sword, will pierce your heart. Many in Israel will stand or fall because of him; and the secret thoughts of many will be laid bare.'

There was also a widow, well advanced in years, who was a prophet. Her name was Anna, the daughter of Phanuel of the tribe of Asher. She had been married for only seven years, and was now eighty-four years old. She never left the temple, serving the Lord day and night with fasting and prayer. She came up at that moment, and gave thanks to God; then she spoke about the child to all who were waiting for Jerusalem to be set free.

When Joseph and Mary had done everything prescribed by the law of the Lord, they returned to their home town of Nazareth in Galilee. The child grew big and strong, and was filled with wisdom; and God's favour was upon him.

Luke 2.33–40

Jesus among the teachers

Every year the parents of Jesus used to go to Jerusalem for the Passover festival. When Jesus was twelve years old, they went to the festival as usual. After the days of the festival were over, they set off home; but the boy Jesus remained in Jerusalem. His parents did not know this; they assumed he was with the group, so they travelled a whole day before they began looking for him among their relatives and friends. When they could not find him, they returned to Jerusalem to search for him there.

Three days later they found him in the temple, sitting among the teachers, listening to them and asking them questions. All who heard him were astounded at his intelligence and the answers he gave. His parents were overcome when they saw him. 'My son,' his mother said, 'why have you treated us like this? Your father and I have been terribly anxious trying to find you.' Jesus said: 'Why were you looking for me? Did you not know that I would be in my Father's house?' But they did not understand what he meant.

Then he went back with them to Nazareth, and continued to live under their authority. His mother treasured all these things in her heart. Jesus grew both in body and in wisdom, gaining favour with God and with people.

Luke 2.41–52

The proclamation of John the Baptist

John the Baptist appeared in the desert of Judaea, and began to preach: 'Repent, for the kingdom of heaven is near.' He wore a rough coat of camel's hair, with a belt round his waist, and he fed on locusts and wild honey. People flocked to him from Jerusalem, Judaea and the Jordan valley. They confessed their sins, and he baptized them in the River Jordan.

When John saw a number of Pharisees and Sadducees coming for baptism, he said to them: 'Brood of vipers! Who warned you to escape from the wrath that is to come? Prove your repentance by the fruit that you bear. Do not tell yourselves, "We have Abraham for our father." I tell you, God can make children for Abraham from these stones. The axe lies ready at the roots of the trees; every tree that does not bear good fruit will be cut down and thrown on the fire.

'I baptize you with water as a sign of repentance; but the one who comes after me will baptize you with the Holy Spirit and with fire. He is much greater than I am; I am not worthy even to carry his sandals.'

Matthew 3. 1–2, 4–11

The baptism of Jesus

Jesus came to the Jordan from Galilee, to be baptized by John. But John tried to dissuade him: 'It is I who needs baptism from you, and yet you come to me!' Jesus replied: 'Let it be so for the present; we do well in this way to do what God requires.' So John agreed.

When Jesus had been baptized and had risen out of the water, the skies opened, and he saw the Spirit of God descending like a dove and coming down on him. And a voice spoke from heaven: 'This is my beloved Son, on whom my favour rests.'

Matthew 3.13−17

The temptation of Jesus

Filled with the Holy Spirit, Jesus returned from the Jordan, and for forty days he wandered in the desert, led by the Spirit and tempted by the devil. During that time he ate nothing, so at the end he was famished.

The devil said to him: 'If you are the Son of God, tell this stone to become bread.' Jesus answered: 'Scripture says, "Humans cannot live on bread alone."'

Then, leading him to a great height, the devil showed him in a flash all the kingdoms of the world. He said: 'I shall give you power over all this, and the glory that goes with it; for it has been put in my hands, to give to anyone I choose. Do homage to me, and it will be yours.' But Jesus answered: 'Scripture says, "Worship the Lord your God, and serve him alone."'

The devil took him to Jerusalem, and set him on the parapet of the temple. He said: 'If you are the Son of God, throw yourself down from here. For Scripture says, "He will put his angels in charge of you," and again, "They will carry you in their arms, for fear you should hit your feet against a stone."' But Jesus answered: 'Scripture says, "Do not put the Lord your God to the test."'

When the devil had finished tempting Jesus in every way, he departed, biding his time.

Luke 4.1–13

Calling the first disciples

Jesus was standing on the shore of Lake Galilee, when he saw two boats at the water's edge. The fishermen had come ashore and were washing their nets. Jesus got into one of the boats, which belonged to Simon, and asked him to push off a little way from the shore.

Then he said to Simon: 'Take the boat into deep water, and let down your nets for a catch.' 'Master,' Simon replied, 'we have worked hard all night long and caught nothing. But, if you say so, we shall let down the nets.' They did so, and caught such a huge number of fish that their nets began to tear. They signalled to their partners in the other boat to come and help them. They came and loaded both boats to the point of sinking.

When Simon saw what had happened, he fell on his knees before Jesus, and said: 'Go, Lord, leave me; I am a sinful man.' He and all his companions were amazed at the catch they had made; so too were his partners James and John, the sons of Zebedee. Jesus said: 'Do not be afraid; from now on you will be catching people.'

They pulled their boats up on the land, left everything, and followed him.

Luke 5. 1—11

The wedding at Cana

Two days later there was a wedding at Cana in Galilee. The mother of Jesus was there, and Jesus and his disciples were also among the guests. The wine ran out, so Jesus's mother said to him: 'They have no wine left.' Jesus replied: 'Your concern, mother, is not mine. My hour has not yet come.' His mother said to the servants: 'Do whatever he tells you.'

There were six stone water jars standing near, to be used for the ablutions which are customary among the people; each could hold twenty or thirty gallons. Jesus said to the servants: 'Fill the jars with water.' The servants filled them to the brim. Then he ordered: 'Now draw some out, and take it to the master of the feast.' They did so. The master tasted the water, which had now turned into wine. The master had no idea where the wine came from, though the servants who had drawn the water knew. He called the bridegroom, and said: 'Everyone else serves the good wine first, and then poorer wine only when the guests have drunk freely; but you have kept the best wine till now.'

So Jesus performed at Cana in Galilee the first of the signs which revealed his glory, and led his disciples to believe in him.

John 2. 1–11

The first healings

Jesus and his disciples came to the town of Capernaum; and on the sabbath he went to the synagogue, and began to teach. The people were astounded at his teaching because, unlike the teachers of the law, he spoke with authority.

A man with an evil spirit was in the synagogue, and screamed at Jesus: 'What do you want with us, Jesus of Nazareth? Have you come to destroy us? I know who you are: the Holy One of God.' Jesus ordered the spirit: 'Be quiet, and come out of the man.' The evil spirit threw the man into convulsions, and with a loud cry left him. The people were amazed. They asked one another: 'What is this? A new kind of teaching? He speaks with authority. Even the evil spirits obey him.' His reputation soon spread far and wide throughout Galilee.

Jesus and his disciples, including James and John, left the synagogue and went to the home of Simon and Andrew. Simon's mother-in-law was in bed with a fever. As soon as they told him about her, he came to her, took her by the hand, and helped her to her feet. The fever left her, and she began to wait on them.

That evening after sunset people brought to Jesus all who were ill or possessed by demons. The whole town gathered at the door of the house. He healed many who were sick with diseases of every kind, and drove out many demons. He would not let the demons speak because they knew who he was.

Mark 1.21–34

A paralyzed man

Early next morning, long before dawn, Jesus got up and left the house. He travelled throughout Galilee, preaching in the synagogues and driving out demons.

After some days he returned to Capernaum, and news spread that he was at home; and so many people gathered there that there was no space for them even outside the door. While he was preaching his message to them, four men arrived, carrying a paralyzed man. Because of the crowd they could not get near Jesus, so they stripped the roof directly above him. And when they had made an opening, they lowered the bed on which the paralyzed man lay. When Jesus saw their faith, he said to the paralyzed man: 'My son, your sins are forgiven.'

Some teachers of the law who were sitting nearby thought: 'How can this man talk like that? It is blasphemy! God alone can forgive sins.' Jesus knew at once what they were thinking. So he said to them: 'Why do you harbour such thoughts? Is it easier to say to a paralyzed man, "Your sins are forgiven" or to say, "Stand up, take your bed and walk"? I shall prove to you that the Son of Man has authority on earth to forgive sins.' He turned to the paralyzed man, and said: 'I order you to stand up, take your bed and walk.' The man rose up, and at once picked up his bed and walked out, in full view of everyone. They were utterly astonished, and praised God, saying: 'Never before have we seen anything like this.'

Mark 1.35a, 39; 2.1–12

Calling Matthew

As Jesus was walking along he saw a man called Matthew sitting at the tax office. Jesus said to him: 'Follow me.' And Matthew got up, and followed him.

While Jesus was having a meal in Matthew's house, many tax collectors and other outcasts came and joined Jesus and his disciples. When the Pharisees saw this, they said to the disciples: 'Why does your teacher eat with such people?' Jesus heard them and answered: 'It is not the healthy man that needs a doctor, but the sick. I have come not to call the virtuous, but outcasts.'

Then John's disciples came to him, and said: 'Why is it that we and the Pharisees fast, but your disciples do not?' Jesus replied: 'Can you expect the bridegroom's friends to be sad while the bridegroom is with them? The time will come when the bridegroom will be taken away from them; then they will fast.'

Jesus continued: 'No one puts a patch of unshrunk cloth on an old garment, because the patch tears from the garment and makes a bigger hole. Nor do people put new wine into old wineskins; if they do, the skins burst, the wine runs out and the skins are ruined. No, they put new wine into fresh wineskins, and both are preserved.'

Matthew 9.9–12, 13b–17

The companions of Jesus

Jesus went onto a mountain to pray and he spent the whole night praying to God. At dawn he called his disciples to him and from among them he chose twelve, naming them apostles. They were Simon, whom he called Peter, and his brother Andrew, James, John, Philip, Bartholomew, Matthew, Thomas, James son of Alphaeus, Simon called the Zealot, Judas son of James and Judas Iscariot who turned traitor.

He then came down from the mountain and stopped on some level ground, where a large crowd of disciples had gathered. With them were great numbers from Jerusalem and all Judaea, and from the coastal region of Tyre and Sidon, who had come to listen to him and be healed of their diseases. Those who were tormented by evil spirits, were cured; and everyone in the crowd was trying to touch him, because power went from him which healed them all.

Jesus continued to travel through towns and villages proclaiming the good news of God's kingdom; and the twelve disciples went with him. He was also accompanied by a number of women who had been healed of evil spirits and illnesses. They included Mary, known as Mary of Magdala, from whom seven demons had come out; Joanna, the wife of one of Herod's stewards called Chuza; and Susanna. They provided for Jesus and the twelve apostles out of their own resources.

Luke 6.12–19; 8.1–3

God's family

Jesus returned home again and once more such a large crowd collected that they could not even have a meal. When his family heard of what was happening, they set out to take charge of him. People were saying: 'He is out of his mind.'

The teachers of the law, who had come from Jerusalem, said: 'He is possessed by Beelzebub. He drives out demons by the prince of demons.' So he called them to him, and spoke to them in parables: 'How can Satan drive out Satan? If a kingdom is divided against itself, that kingdom will fall apart. And if a family is divided against itself, that family will fall apart. So if Satan is divided and rebels against himself, he cannot last either, and that is the end of him. No one can break into a strong man's house and steal his goods, unless he has first tied up the strong man. Only then can he ransack his house. In truth I tell you, every sin and every slander can be forgiven; but anyone who slanders the Holy Spirit is guilty of an eternal sin, and can never be forgiven.'

His mother and brothers arrived, and sent a message into the house asking for him. The crowd was sitting round him, when the message was brought that his mother and brothers were outside asking for him. 'Who are my mother and my brothers?' he asked. And looking at those sitting in a circle round him, he said: 'Here are my mother and my brothers. Anyone who does the will of God is my brother and sister and mother.'

Mark 3.20–29, 31–35

Nicodemus

A Pharisee called Nicodemus, a leader of the people, came to Jesus by night. 'Master,' he said, 'we know that you are a teacher sent by God; no one could perform the signs that you do unless God were with him.' Jesus answered: 'You cannot see the kingdom of God unless you have been born again.' Nicodemus asked: 'But how can someone be born who is already old? Is it possible to return to the womb, and be born a second time?' Jesus said: 'You cannot enter the kingdom of God without being born from water and the Spirit. Flesh can give birth only to flesh; but the Spirit gives birth to spirit. Do not be surprised when I say that you must all be born again. The wind blows where it wishes; you hear its sound, but you cannot tell where it comes from or where it is going. So it is with everyone who is born of the Spirit.'

'How is this possible?' asked Nicodemus. Jesus replied: 'You are a teacher of Israel, and ignorant of these things! In all truth I tell you, we speak of what we know, and testify to what we have seen, and yet you reject our testimony. If you do not believe me when I talk about earthly things, how will you believe me when I talk about the things of heaven? No one has gone up to heaven except the Son of Man who came down from heaven.

'God so loved the world that he gave his only Son, so all who believe in him may not die, but have eternal life. God sent his Son into the world not to be its judge, but to be its saviour.'

John 3.1–13, 16–17

The Beatitudes

Jesus again went up the mountain. There he sat down, and when his disciples had gathered round him he began to teach them:

'Blessed are the poor in spirit; the kingdom of heaven is theirs.

'Blessed are those who mourn; they will be comforted.

'Blessed are those of gentle spirit; they will possess the earth.

'Blessed are those who hunger and thirst to see right prevail; they will be satisfied.

'Blessed are those who show mercy; they will have mercy shown to them.

'Blessed are those whose hearts are pure; they will see God.

'Blessed are the peacemakers; they will be called children of God.

'Blessed are those who are persecuted in the cause of right; the kingdom of heaven is theirs.

'Blessed are you, when people abuse you and persecute you and speak all kinds of falsehoods against you for my sake. Rejoice and be glad, for you have a rich reward in heaven; they persecuted the prophets in the same way before you.'

Matthew 5.1–12

Salt and light

'You are salt to the world. But if salt loses its taste, how can it be made salty again? It is good for nothing, but to be thrown away and trampled underfoot.

'You are light for the world. A city built on a hilltop cannot be hidden. When a lamp is lit, it is not put under a tub, but on a lamp-stand, where it shines for everyone in the house. In the same way your light must shine among people, so that, seeing your good works, they may give praise to your Father in heaven.

'Do not think that I have come to abolish the law and the prophets; I have not come to abolish, but to fulfil them. In truth I tell you, so long as heaven and earth endure, not a letter, not a dot, will disappear from the law until all its purpose is achieved. Thus anyone who sets aside even the least of the law's commands, and teaches others to do the same, will have the lowest place in the kingdom of heaven. But the person who keeps them and teaches them, will be considered great in the kingdom of heaven.'

Matthew 5.13–19

Anger and conflict

'You have heard that it was said to our ancestors: "Do not kill; murderers must be brought to justice." But I say to you, anyone who nurses anger against his brother must be brought to justice; anyone who calls a brother "good for nothing" deserves the sentence of the court; and anyone who calls him "fool" deserves the fire of hell. So if you are offering your gift at the altar and remember that your brother has a grievance against you, leave your gift before the altar, go and make peace with your brother, and then come back and offer the gift.

'If people sue you, come to terms with them promptly while on your way to the court, or they may hand you over to the judge, and the judge to the officer, and you will be thrown into jail. In truth I tell you, you will not get out until you have paid the fine in full.'

Matthew 5.21–26

Adultery and divorce

'You have heard that it was said: "Do not commit adultery."
But I say to you, if a man looks at a woman with a lustful
eye, he has already committed adultery with her in his heart.
If your right eye causes your downfall, tear it out and throw
it away; it is better for you to lose one part of your body,
than for your whole body to be thrown into hell. If your
right hand causes your downfall, cut it off and throw it away;
it is better to lose one part of your body, than for it all to be
thrown into hell.

'It was also said: "A man who divorces his wife must give
her a note of dismissal." But I say to you, a man who divorces his wife, except on the ground of unchastity, makes
her guilty of adultery if she marries again; and whoever marries her also commits adultery.'

Matthew 5.27–32

Honesty and reconciliation

'Again, you have heard that it was said to our ancestors: "Do not break your oath, but keep oaths sworn to the Lord." But I say to you, do not swear at all, either by heaven, since that is God's throne, or by earth, since that is his footstool, or by Jerusalem, since that is the city of the great king. Do not swear by your own head either, since you cannot turn a single hair white or black. Plain "Yes" or "No" is all you need to say; anything beyond that comes from the Evil One.

'You heard that it was said: "An eye for an eye, a tooth for a tooth." But I say to you, do not resist those who wrong you. If anyone slaps you on the right cheek, turn and offer the other also. If anyone wishes to sue you and takes your shirt, let him have your cloak as well. If someone forces you to go one mile, go two miles. Give to anyone who asks you; and if anyone wants to borrow, do not turn your back.

'You have heard that it was said: "Love your neighbour and hate your enemy." But I say to you, love your enemies and pray for those who persecute you; thus you may be children of your Father in heaven, who causes the sun to rise on good and bad alike, and sends the rain on the innocent and the wicked. If you love only those who love you, what reward can you expect? Even the tax collectors do as much. If you speak only to your friends, what is exceptional about that? Even the heathens do as much. You must be perfect, as your Father in heaven is perfect.'

Matthew 5.33–48

True religion

'Be careful not to parade your religion before others; if you do, you will have no reward from your Father in heaven.

'So when you give help to someone in need, do not announce it with a flourish of trumpets; that is what the hypocrites do in synagogues and in the streets to win praise. In truth I tell you, they have their reward already. When you give help, do not let your left hand know what your right hand is doing. Your good deed must be secret; and your Father, who sees what is done in secret, will reward you.

'When you pray, do not be like the hypocrites; they love to say their prayers standing up in synagogues and at street corners, for people to see them. In truth I tell you, they have their reward. But when you pray, go into a room by yourself, shut the door, and pray to your Father who is in that secret place; and your Father who sees what is done in secret, will reward you.

'In your prayers do not babble like the heathen, who imagine that the more they say, the more likely they are to be heard. Do not be like them, for your Father knows what you need before you ask him.'

Matthew 6. 1–8

True prayer

'This is how you should pray: "Our Father in heaven, hallowed be your name; your kingdom come, your will be done, on earth as in heaven. Give us today our daily bread. Forgive us our sins, as we forgive those who sin against us. Lead us not into temptation, but deliver us from evil."

'If you forgive others the sins they have committed, your heavenly Father will also forgive you; but if you do not forgive others, then your Father will not forgive your sins.

'When you fast, do not look gloomy like the hypocrites; they make their faces unsightly to show people they are fasting. In truth I tell you, they have their reward. But when you fast, anoint your head and wash your face, so that no one sees you are fasting except your Father, who sees what is done in secret; and your Father, who is unseen, will reward you.

'Do not store up for yourselves treasure on earth, where moths and rust destroy, and thieves break in and steal. But store up treasure in heaven, where neither moths nor rust can destroy, nor thieves break in and steal. For where your treasure is, there also will be your heart.'

Matthew 6.9–21

Persistence in prayer

'Suppose that you were to go to a friend's house in the middle of the night and say: "My friend, let me borrow three loaves of bread. A friend of mine has just arrived at my house, and I have no food for him." And suppose that the man were to shout back from inside the house: "Do not bother me. The door is already bolted, and my children and I are in bed. I cannot get up and give you anything." I tell you that even if he will not get up and give you the bread for the sake of friendship, persistence on your part will force him to get up and give you what you want.

'And so I say to you, ask and you will receive; seek and you will find; knock and the door will be opened to you. Everyone who asks receives; those who seek find; and to those who knock, the door will be opened.

'Would any father among you offer his son a snake when he asks for a fish, or a scorpion when he asks for an egg? If you, bad as you are, know how to give good things to your children, how much more will your Father in heaven give the Holy Spirit to those who ask him.'

Luke 11.5–13

God and money

'No one can serve two masters: either he will hate the one and love the other, or he will be devoted to the one and despise the other. You cannot serve both God and money.

'That is why I tell you not to be anxious about food and drink to keep you alive, and about clothes to cover your body. Is not life more than food, and the body more than clothes? Look at the birds in the sky: they do not sow or reap or store in barns, yet your heavenly Father feeds them. Are you not worth more than the birds? Can anxious thoughts add a single day to your life? And why be anxious about clothes? Consider how the lilies grow in the field: they neither work nor spin; yet I tell you, even Solomon in all his splendour was not clothed like one of them. If that is how God clothes the grass in the fields, which is there today and thrown on the stove tomorrow, will he not all the more clothe you? How little faith you have! Do not ask anxiously: "What are we to eat? What are we to drink? What shall we wear?" The heathen set their hearts on these things. But your heavenly Father knows that you need them all. Set your hearts first on God's kingdom and his justice, and all these things will be yours as well.

'So do not be anxious about tomorrow; tomorrow will look after itself. Each day has troubles enough of its own.'

Matthew 6.24–34

Goodness and humility

'Do not judge, and you will not be judged. Do not condemn, and you will not be condemned. Forgive, and you will be forgiven. Give, and there will be gifts for you: a full measure, pressed and shaken down, and running over, will be poured into your lap. Whatever measure you deal out to others will in turn be dealt to you.

'Can one blind person guide another? Will not both fall into the ditch? Pupils cannot rank above their teacher; when they are fully trained they will reach their teacher's level.

'Why do you look at the speck in your brother's eye, but do not notice the log in your own eye? How can you say to your brother, "Let me take the speck out of your eye," when you are blind to the log in your own eye? First take the log out of your own eye, and then you will see clearly to take the speck out of your brother's eye.

'A healthy tree cannot produce bad fruit, nor a rotten tree good fruit. Good people produce good out of the store of good within themselves; and evil people produce evil from the evil within them. The words that come out of the mouth flow from the heart.'

Luke 6.37–43, 45

True authority

'Always do to others as you would wish them to do to you; that is the law and the prophets.

'Enter by the narrow gate. The gate is wide and the road broad that lead to destruction, and many go that way. But the gate is narrow and the road hard that lead to life, and few find them.

'Not everyone who says to me, "Lord, Lord" will enter the kingdom of heaven, but only those who do the will of my heavenly Father. When the day comes, many will say to me: "Lord, Lord, did we not prophesy in your name, drive out demons in your name, and in your name perform many miracles?" Then I shall tell them plainly: "I never knew you. Out of my sight; your deeds are evil."

'Whoever hears these words of mine and acts on them, is like a wise man who built his house on rock. Rain came down, floods rose and gales blew, battering that house; but it did not fall, because its foundations were on rock. And whoever hears these words of mine and does not act on them, is like a foolish man who built his house on sand. Rain came down, floods rose and gales blew, battering that house; and it fell with a great crash.'

When Jesus finished speaking, the people were amazed at his teaching; unlike their teachers of the law he taught with a note of authority.

Matthew 7.12−14, 21−29

A centurion's servant

When Jesus came down from the mountain, large crowds followed him. A man with leprosy approached him, and knelt at his feet. 'Sir,' the leper said, 'if you are willing, you can make me clean.' Jesus stretched out his hand and touched him, saying: 'I am willing; be clean.' At once the leprosy was cured. Then Jesus said to him: 'See that you tell nobody. But go straight to the priest and let him examine you; then make the offering laid down by Moses to certify the cure.'

As Jesus entered Capernaum a centurion came up to ask his help. 'Sir,' he pleaded, 'my servant is lying at home, paralyzed and racked with pain.' 'I shall come and cure him,' Jesus said. 'Sir,' the centurion replied, 'I am not worthy to have you under my roof; just give the word and my servant will be healed. I am under authority myself, and have soldiers under me: I say to one man, "Go," and he goes; to another, "Come here," and he comes; to my servant, "Do this," and he does it.'

Jesus was astonished as he heard this, and said to the people following him: 'In truth I tell you, nowhere in Israel have I found such faith. Many, I tell you, will come from east and west to sit down with Abraham, Isaac and Jacob at the feast in the kingdom of heaven. But those who were born to the kingdom will be thrown out into the dark, where there will be weeping and grinding of teeth.' Then Jesus said to the centurion: 'Go home; according to your faith, let it be done.'

Matthew 8.1–13

A woman with haemorrhages

Jesus returned by boat to the other side of the lake, where a large crowd gathered round him. Jairus, the president of the local synagogue, arrived. Seeing Jesus, he fell at his feet, crying: 'My little daughter is at death's door. I beg you to come and lay your hands on her, so that her life may be saved.' So Jesus went with him, accompanied by a large crowd that pressed round him.

Among the people was a woman who had suffered from haemorrhages for twelve years. She had been treated by many doctors, and spent all she had, but had become worse rather than better. She had heard about Jesus; and she came up behind him and touched his cloak, thinking: 'If only I can touch his clothes, I shall be saved.' At once the flow of blood dried up, and she knew within herself that she was healed of her trouble. Jesus felt that power had gone out of him, so he turned round in the crowd, and asked: 'Who touched my clothes?' His disciples said to him: 'You see the crowd pressing round you, and yet you ask who touched you!' But he continued looking all around to see who had done it. Then the woman, trembling with fear because she knew what had happened to her, came forward. She fell at his feet and told him the whole truth. 'Daughter,' he said, 'your faith has healed you. Go in peace, and be free of your trouble.'

Mark 5.21–34

The daughter of Jairus

While Jesus was still speaking, messengers came from Jairus's house, and said to him: 'Your daughter has died. Why bother the Master any longer?' But Jesus, overhearing the message, said to Jairus: 'Do not be afraid; only believe.' He allowed no one to go with him except Peter, James and John the brother of James. They arrived at Jairus's house, where Jesus found a great commotion, with loud weeping and wailing. So he went in, and said: 'Why is there such a commotion? Why are you crying? The child is not dead; she is only sleeping.' They laughed at him, so he turned them out. He led the child's father and mother and his own disciples into the room where the child lay. Taking her by the hand, he said to her, 'Talitha cum', which means, 'Get up, my child'. At once the girl rose up and started to walk about. She was twelve years old. They were overcome with astonishment; but he gave them strict orders not to let anyone know about it. Then he told them to give her something to eat.

From there he went with his disciples to his home town. When the sabbath came, he began to teach in the synagogue. The large crowd who heard him asked in amazement: 'Where did he get all this? What is this wisdom that has been given to him? Is he not a carpenter, the son of Mary, the brother of James, Joseph, Judas and Simon? Are not his sisters here with us?' So they turned against him. Jesus said to them: 'A prophet is honoured everywhere except in his own country, among his own relatives and in his own family.'

Mark 5.35—6.4

Jesus, John and the people

The disciples of John the Baptist told him of all that Jesus had been doing and saying. John summoned two of them, and sent them to the Lord to ask: 'Are you the one who is to come, or are we to expect someone else?'

When the messengers arrived, Jesus was curing many people of diseases, plagues and evil spirits, and giving sight to many who were blind. So he said to John's messengers: 'Go back and tell John what you have seen and heard: the blind see again, the lame walk, lepers are made clean, the deaf hear, the dead are raised to life and good news is proclaimed to the poor. Blessed is the person who does not find me an obstacle to faith.'

After John's messengers had gone, Jesus began to speak about him to the people: 'What did you go into the desert to see? A reed swaying in the wind? No? Then what did you go out to see? A man dressed in fine clothes? Those who dress in grand clothes and live in luxury are to be found in palaces. But what did you go out to see? A prophet? Yes indeed, and far more than a prophet. I tell you, among all who have ever lived, no one is greater than John. Yet the one who is lowest in the kingdom of God is greater than he is.'

Luke 7.18–26, 28

The woman at the well

News reached the Pharisees that Jesus was winning and baptizing more disciples than John – although in fact it was his
disciples, not Jesus himself, who were baptizing. When Jesus
heard this, he left Judaea and set out once more for Galilee.
He had to pass through Samaria, and he came to a Samaritan
town called Sychar, near the land that Jacob gave to his son
Joseph. Jacob's well was there. It was about noon; and Jesus,
tired by the journey, sat down by the well.

His disciples had gone into the town to buy food. Meanwhile a Samaritan woman came to draw water, and Jesus said
to her: 'Give me a drink.' The woman said: 'You are a Jew,
and I am a Samaritan; so how can you ask me for a drink?'
Jews do not share cups and bowls with Samaritans. Jesus
replied: 'If only you knew what God is offering, and who it
is that is asking for a drink, you would ask him, and he
would give you living water.' She said: 'You have no bucket,
sir, and the well is deep, so how can you get this living
water? Are you greater than our ancestor Jacob, who gave us
this well and drank from it himself with his sons and cattle?'
Jesus answered: 'Whoever drinks this water will be thirsty
again; but whoever drinks the water I shall give will never
again be thirsty. The water that I shall give will become an
inner spring, welling up and bringing eternal life.' 'Sir,' said
the woman, 'give me this water so that I may never be
thirsty, nor have to come all this way to draw water.'

John 4.1–15

True worship

Jesus said to the Samaritan woman: 'Go and call your husband and come back here.' 'I have no husband,' she answered. Jesus said: 'You are right in saying you have no husband, for although you have had five husbands, the man you are living with now is not your husband. You have spoken the truth.' 'Sir,' replied the woman, 'I see you are a prophet. Our ancestors worshipped on the mountain, but you Jews say that God should be worshipped in Jerusalem.' Jesus said: 'Believe me, the time is coming when you will worship the Father neither on the mountain nor in Jerusalem. You Samaritans worship without knowing what you worship, while we worship what we know, because salvation comes from the Jews. But the time is coming, indeed it is already here, when true worshippers will worship the Father in spirit and in truth. These are the worshippers the Father wants. God is spirit, and those who worship him must worship in spirit and in truth.'

The woman said: 'I know that Christ is coming; and when he comes he will make all things clear to us.' Jesus said: 'I am he – I who am talking with you.'

At that moment his disciples returned, and were astonished to find him talking with a woman. But none of them said, 'What do you want from her?' or, 'Why are you talking with her?' The woman put down her water jar and hurried back to the town, where she said to the people: 'Come and see a man who had told me everything I ever did. Could this be the Christ?'

John 4.16–29

The death of John

At around this time Herod sent men to arrest John, put him in chains and throw him in prison. He did this at the insistence of Herodias, his brother Philip's wife whom he had married. John had told Herod: 'You have no right to take your brother's wife.' So Herodias nursed a grudge against John and wanted to kill him; but she was restrained because Herod, knowing John to be a good and holy man, stood in awe of him and protected him. Herod liked to listen to John, although his words deeply disturbed him.

Herodias found her opportunity when Herod on his birthday gave a banquet to his chief officials and military commanders and the leading citizens of Galilee. Her daughter came in and danced. Herod and his guests were so delighted that the king said to the girl: 'Ask me for anything you like and I shall give it to you.' He even swore an oath: 'Whatever you ask, I shall give you, up to half my kingdom.' She went out, and said to her mother: 'What shall I ask for?' Her mother replied: 'The head of John the Baptist.' The girl hurried back to the king and demanded: 'I want you to give me, here and now, the head of John the Baptist on a dish.'

The king was greatly distressed; but because of the oath he had sworn in front of his guests, he could not refuse her. He sent off a guard with orders to bring John's head. The guard went to the prison and beheaded John. Then he returned with the head on a dish and gave it to the girl; and she gave it to her mother.

When John's disciples heard the news, they came and took his body away, and laid it in a tomb.

Mark 6.17–29

Martha and Mary

While he was on his way, Jesus came to a village where a
woman named Martha welcomed him into her house. She
had a sister called Mary, who sat down at the Lord's feet and
listened to his words. Martha was distracted by her various
tasks, so she came to Jesus, and said: 'Do you not care, Lord,
that my sister is leaving me with all the work? Please tell her
to help me.' But the Lord answered: 'Martha, Martha, you
worry and fret about so many things, yet only one thing is
necessary. Mary has chosen what is best, and it will not be
taken away from her.'

Luke 10.38–42

The sower and the seeds

Jesus began to teach the people beside Lake Galilee: 'A sower went out to sow. As he scattered the seed, some fell along the path, and the birds came and ate it up. Some fell on rocky ground where there was little soil, and it quickly sprouted because it had no depth of earth; but when the sun came up it was scorched, and, as it had no root, it withered away. Some fell among thistles; and the thistles grew up and choked it, and it produced no crop. And some of the seed fell on good soil, where it grew tall and strong and produced a crop; the yield was thirty, sixty and even a hundredfold.' And he added: 'If you have ears to hear, then hear.'

When Jesus was alone, the twelve apostles and some other companions questioned him about the parable. He replied: 'The sower sows God's word. People on the path hear the word. But at once Satan comes and carries off what is sown within them. People on rocky ground hear the word, and accept it with joy. But it takes no root within them, so it cannot last: when trouble or persecution comes on account of the word, they quickly lose faith. People on ground where thistles grow, hear the word. But worldly cares, the lure of wealth and evil passions of all kinds, come in to choke the word, and it produces no crop. People on rich soil hear the word and accept it; and they yield an abundant harvest, thirty, sixty and a hundredfold.'

Mark 4.1a, 3–10, 14–20

Parables of the kingdom

Jesus gave the people further parables: 'The kingdom of heaven is like a mustard seed which a man took and sowed in his field. It is the smallest of all seeds; but when it has grown it is taller than other plants, becoming a tree big enough for birds to come and roost among its branches.

'The kingdom of heaven is like yeast which a woman takes and mixes with three measures of flour until it has all risen.

'The kingdom of heaven is like treasure which a man finds buried in a field. He buries it again; and, filled with joy, he goes off and sells everything he owns, in order to buy the field.

'The kingdom of heaven is like a merchant looking for fine pearls. When he finds one of great value, he goes and sells everything he owns to buy it.

'Again, the kingdom of heaven is like a net cast into the sea, where it catches every kind of fish. When it is full, the men haul it ashore; then they sit down and collect the good fish into baskets, throwing the worthless ones away.'

Matthew 13.31–33, 44–48

The mission of the apostles

Jesus went round all the towns and villages, teaching in the synagogues, proclaiming the good news of the kingdom and curing every kind of disease and sickness. As he saw the crowds, his heart was filled with pity, because they were like sheep without a shepherd, harassed and helpless. He said to his disciples: 'The crop is heavy, but the labourers are few; ask the owner for labourers to bring in the harvest.'

Then he summoned his twelve disciples together, and sent them out with these instructions: 'Do not go to Gentile territory or to Samaritan towns, but go rather to the lost sheep of the house of Israel. And as you go, proclaim that the kingdom of heaven is close at hand. Heal the sick, raise the dead, cleanse lepers and drive out demons. You have received without cost, so give without charge. Take no gold, silver or copper in your belts, no pack for the journey, no spare coat or sandals, and no staff; the worker deserves his keep.

'Whatever town or village you enter, seek out some suitable person, and stay with him until you leave. When you go into a house, say: "Peace be with you." If the people in that house welcome you, let your peace come upon it; but if not, let your peace come back to you. If anyone does not receive you or listen to what you say then, as you leave that house or that town, shake the dust of it off your feet.'

Matthew 9.35–38, 10.1a, 5–14

Sheep among wolves

Jesus continued: 'I send you out like sheep among wolves; be wary as snakes, and innocent as doves.

'Be on your guard, for you will be handed over to the courts, and flogged in the synagogues. You will be brought before governors and kings for my sake, to testify before them and the Gentiles. But when you are arrested, do not worry about how to speak or what to say. When the time comes, the words you need will be given to you; for it will not be you speaking, but the Spirit of your Father speaking in you.

'Brother will betray brother to death, and a father his child; children will turn against their parents and send them to their death. All will hate you for your allegiance to me; but whoever stands firm to the end will be saved. If you are persecuted in one town, take refuge in the next. In truth I tell you, you will not have gone through all the towns of Israel before the Son of Man comes.

'No pupil is superior to his teacher, no servant to his master. It is enough for the pupil to become like his teacher, the servant like his master. If the master has been called Beelzebub, members of his household will be called even worse names.'

Matthew 10.16–25

The sword of faith

'Do not be afraid of people. Whatever is now covered up, will be uncovered; and what is now hidden will be made known. What I say to you in the dark, you must repeat in broad daylight; what you hear whispered, you must shout from the housetops. Do not fear those who kill the body but cannot kill the soul. Rather fear those who can destroy both body and soul in hell. Can you not buy two sparrows for a single coin? And yet not one of them falls to the ground without your Father's leave. As for you, even the hairs on your head have all been counted. So do not be afraid: you are worth more than any number of sparrows.

'Those who acknowledge me before other human beings, I shall acknowledge before my Father in heaven. But those who disown me before others, I shall disown before my Father in heaven.

'Do not think that I have come to bring peace to the earth; I have come not to bring peace, but a sword. I have come to set a son against his father, a daughter against her mother, a young wife against her mother-in-law; people will find enemies within their own families.

'Those who love father or mother more than me, are not worthy of me. Those who love son or daughter more than me, are not worthy of me. Those who do not take up their cross and follow in my footsteps, are not worthy of me. Those who try to gain their own life, will lose it; but those who lose their life for my sake, will gain it.

Matthew 10.26–39

A Canaanite woman

Jesus and his disciples left that place, and went to the region of Tyre and Sidon. A Canaanite woman who lived there, came to meet him. 'Son of David,' she cried, 'have pity on me. My daughter is tormented by a devil.' But Jesus did not reply. His disciples came and pleaded with him: 'Give her what she wants, because she keeps shouting after us.' Jesus replied: 'I was sent only to the lost sheep of Israel.' At this the woman fell at his feet, pleading: 'Lord, help me.' Jesus answered: 'It is not right to take the children's bread, and throw it to the dogs.' She retorted: 'True, Lord, but even dogs eat the scraps that fall from their master's table.' Hearing these words, Jesus exclaimed: 'Woman, you have great faith. Let your wish be granted.' And at that moment her daughter was restored to health.

Matthew 15.21–28

A cripple at Bethesda

Jesus now went up to Jerusalem for one of the Jewish festivals. Near the Sheep Gate in Jerusalem is a pool called in Hebrew Bethesda. Under its five porticoes lay a large number of sick people, some blind, others lame or paralyzed. Among them was a man who had been crippled for thirty-eight years. Jesus saw him lying there; and, knowing that he had been ill for so long, asked him: 'Do you want to get well?' 'Sir,' he replied, 'I have no one to put me into the pool when the water is stirred up; and, while I am getting there, someone always steps in first.' Jesus said: 'Stand up, take your mat and walk.' The man recovered instantly; he picked up his mat and started walking.

The day this occurred was a sabbath. So the people said to the man who had been healed: 'It is the sabbath; it is against the law to carry your mat.' He answered: 'The man who cured me told me to pick up my mat and walk.' 'Who is the man who told you to do this?' they asked. But the man who had been cured did not know who Jesus was; and Jesus had slipped away through the crowds.

A little later Jesus found the man in the temple, and said to him: 'Now that you are well, give up your sinful ways, or something worse may happen to you.' The man went off and told the Jewish authorities that it was Jesus who had healed him.

John 5.1–15

A woman caught in adultery

Early next morning Jesus appeared again in the temple. People gathered round him, and he sat down and began to teach them. The teachers of the law and Pharisees brought in a woman who had been caught committing adultery, and made her stand in the middle. 'Master,' they said to Jesus, 'this woman was caught in the very act of adultery, and the law of Moses lays down that such women must be stoned. What have you got to say?' They put this question to test him, hoping to frame a charge against him. Jesus bent down and started writing with his finger on the ground. When they pressed their question, he sat up straight, and said: 'Let one of you who is free from sin cast the first stone.' Then he bent down again and continued writing on the ground.

When they heard what he said, they went away one by one, the eldest first. Jesus was left alone with the woman, who was still standing in the middle. Jesus again sat up. 'Where are they? Has no one condemned you?' he asked the woman. 'No one, sir,' she answered. Jesus said: 'Neither do I condemn you; go and do not sin again.'

John 8.2–12

The good shepherd

Jesus said: 'In all truth I tell you, I am the gate of the sheep-fold. All who have come before me, were thieves and robbers, but the sheep took no notice of them. I am the gate. Those who come into the fold through me, will be safe; they will come in and go out, and will find pasture. A thief comes only to steal, kill and destroy; I have come that they may have life, and have it to the full.

'I am the good shepherd; the good shepherd lays down his life for his sheep. The hired man, when he sees the wolf coming, abandons the sheep and runs away, because he is not the shepherd, and the sheep are not his; then the wolf attacks the sheep and scatters them. The man runs away because he is hired, and cares nothing for the sheep.

'I am the good shepherd. As the Father knows me and I know the Father, so I know my sheep and my sheep know me; and I lay down my life for the sheep. There are other sheep of mine not belonging to this fold; I must lead them also. They too will listen to my voice, and there will be one flock with one shepherd.'

John 10.7–16

A woman with a bad name

A Pharisee invited Jesus to a meal. When Jesus arrived at the Pharisee's house and took his place at table, a woman with a bad name in the town came in. She had heard that Jesus was dining there, and she brought with her an alabaster jar containing oil of myrrh. She knelt behind him at his feet, and wept. Her tears fell on his feet, and she wiped them away with her hair. Then she kissed his feet and anointed them with the myrrh.

When the Pharisee saw this, he said to himself: 'If this man were a real prophet, he would know the sort of woman she is who is touching him, and what a bad name she has.'

Pointing to the woman, Jesus said to the Pharisee, who was called Simon: 'Do you see this woman? I came to your house. You provided no water for my feet; but this woman has washed my feet with her tears, and wiped them with her hair. You gave me no kiss; but she has been covering my feet with kisses ever since I arrived. You did not anoint my head with oil; but she has anointed my feet with myrrh. So, I tell you, the great love that she has shown proves that her sins, many as they are, have been forgiven. Where little has been forgiven, little love is shown.'

Then he said to the woman: 'Your sins are forgiven.' The other guests began to ask themselves: 'Who is this, that he can forgive sins?' But he said to her: 'Your faith has saved you; go in peace.'

Luke 7.36–39, 44–50

True hospitality

One sabbath Jesus went to have a meal in the house of one of the leading Pharisees; and people were watching him closely. He noticed how the guests were choosing the places of honour. So he said: 'When someone invites you to a wedding feast, do not sit down in the place of honour. A more distinguished person may have been invited, and the host will come and say to you: "Give up your place to this man." Then you will look foolish as you go and take the lowest place. Instead, when you are a guest, go and sit down at the lowest place, so when your host comes he will say: "My friend, come up higher." Then the people with you at the table will see the respect in which you are held. Those who exalt themselves will be humbled; and those who humble themselves, will be exalted.'

Then Jesus said to his host: 'When you are having guests for lunch or supper, do not invite your friends, your brothers or other relations, or rich neighbours; they will repay you by inviting you back. When you give a party, ask the poor, the crippled, the lame and the blind. Then you will be blessed, because they cannot repay you. You will be repaid when the people of goodness rise to life.'

Luke 14.1, 7–14

The great feast

Hearing the words of Jesus about hospitality, one of those at table with him said: 'Blessed are those who will sit at the feast in the kingdom of God.' Jesus said to him: 'A man was giving a great feast, and invited a large number of people. At dinner time he sent his servant to say to his guests: "Come, everything is now ready." One after another they made excuses. The first said: "I have bought a piece of land, and must go and inspect it; please accept my apologies." The second said: "I have bought five pairs of oxen, and am on my way to try them out; please accept my apologies." The next said: "I cannot come because I have just got married."

'The servant returned and reported this to his master. The master of the house was furious, and said to him: "Go out quickly into the streets and alleys of the town, and bring back the poor, the crippled, the blind and the lame." The servant soon informed him that his orders had been carried out, and there was still room. So the master said to the servant: "Go to the country roads and to the hedgerows, and press people to come in; I want my house full. I tell you, not one of those who were invited shall taste my banquet."'

Luke 14.15–24

Marriage and children

Jesus came into the region of Judaea on the other side of the river Jordan. Again crowds gathered round him, and, according to his custom, he taught them. He was asked: 'Is it lawful for a man to divorce his wife?' This question was put to test him. He responded by asking: 'What did Moses command you?' They replied: 'Moses permitted a man to divorce his wife by a note of dismissal.' Jesus said to them: 'It was because of your hardness of heart that he made this rule for you. But from the beginning of creation God made both male and female. That is why a man leaves his father and mother, and unites with his wife, and the two become one flesh. They are no longer two, but one. Therefore what God has joined together, human beings must not divide.'

When they were indoors, the disciples questioned Jesus about this. He said to them: 'Whoever divorces his wife and marries another woman, commits adultery against his wife. In the same way, a woman who divorces her husband and marries another man, commits adultery.'

People brought children for him to touch. The disciples scolded them. But when Jesus saw this, he was indignant, and said to them: 'Let the children come to me, and do not try to stop them, because the kingdom of God belongs to such as these. In truth I tell you, whoever does not accept the kingdom of God like a child, will never enter it.' Then he put his arms round them, and blessed them.

Mark 10.1–16

The good Samaritan

A teacher of the law came forward to test Jesus. 'Master,' he asked, 'what must I do to inherit eternal life?' Jesus replied: 'What is written in the law? What is your reading of it?' The teacher of the law said: 'Love the Lord your God with all your heart, with all your soul, with all your strength, and with all your mind; and love your neighbour as yourself.' Jesus said: 'That is the right answer; do this and you will have life.'

But the teacher of the law wanted to justify his question, so he asked: 'Who is my neighbour?' Jesus replied: 'A man was on his way from Jerusalem to Jericho when he was attacked by robbers, who stripped and beat him, and left him half dead. A priest happened to be travelling down the same road; but, when he saw the man, he passed by on the other side. A Levite also came to that place and saw him, and passed by on the other side. But a Samaritan travelling that way saw him, and his heart filled with pity. He went up, bathed his wounds in oil and wine, and bandaged them. Then he lifted him onto his own animal, and brought him to an inn where he looked after him. Next day he took out two silver coins, and gave them to the innkeeper, saying: "Care for him; and, if you spend more, I shall repay you on my way back."'

Jesus asked the teacher of the law: 'Which of these three, in your opinion, was neighbour to the man who was attacked by robbers?' 'The one who showed him kindness,' he answered. Jesus said: 'Go, and do as he did.'

Luke 10.25–37

The rich fool

A person in the crowd said to Jesus: 'Master, tell my brother to divide the family property with me.' 'My friend,' Jesus answered, 'who set me over you to judge or arbitrate?' Then he turned to the people, and said: 'Beware! Be on your guard against greed of every kind, because true life does not consist in possessions, even for someone who has more than enough.'

Jesus told them a parable: 'A rich man had a rich harvest from his land. He asked himself: "What am I to do? I have not enough room to store my crop." Then he said: "This is what I shall do: I shall pull down my barns and build bigger ones, and store all my grain and my possessions in them. And I shall assure myself that I have plenty of good things laid by for many years to come – so I can take life easy, eating, drinking and enjoying myself." But God said to him: "You fool, this very night you must surrender your soul. And as for the wealth you have hoarded, who will get it now?"

'That is how it is with those who store up treasure for themselves, and yet remain poor in the sight of God.'

Luke 12.13–21

True wealth

Jesus was starting on his way when a man ran up, knelt before him, and asked: 'Good Master, what I must I do to win eternal life?' Jesus said to him: 'Why do you call me good? No one is good except God alone. You know the commandments: do not murder, do not commit adultery, do not steal, do not accuse anyone falsely, do not cheat, honour your father and mother.' 'Master,' the man said, 'I have kept all these commandments since I was a boy.' As Jesus looked at him, his heart warmed to him and he said: 'You need to do one thing more: go, sell all you have, and give the money to the poor – and you will have treasure in heaven. Then come and follow me.' At these words the man's face fell, and he went away with a heavy heart, for he possessed great wealth.

Jesus looked round, and said to his disciples: 'How hard it is for the rich to enter the kingdom of God.' They were astonished at this, but Jesus insisted: 'Children, how hard it is to enter the kingdom of God! It is easier for a camel to pass through the eye of a needle than for a rich person to enter the kingdom of God.' They were more amazed than ever, and said to one another: 'In that case, who can be saved?' Jesus gazed straight at them, and said: 'For human beings it is impossible, but not for God; everything is possible for God.'

Mark 10.17–27

The workers in the vineyard

Jesus said: 'The kingdom of heaven is like this. A landowner went out early one morning to hire workers for his vineyard. He agreed to pay them one silver coin a day, and sent them off to his vineyard. Three hours later he went out again, and saw some more men standing idle in the market-place. He said to them: "Go and join the others in the vineyard, and I shall pay you a fair wage." So they went. At midday, in the middle of the afternoon, and an hour before dusk, he went out again, and did the same.

'In the evening the owner of the vineyard said to his bailiff: "Call the workers and give them their wages, beginning with those who came last and ending with the first." Those who had started work an hour before sunset, came forward, and were paid a full day's wage. When the first came, they expected more, but were paid the same as the others. As they took their wage, they grumbled to the landowner: "These latecomers did only one hour's work; yet you have treated them the same as us, though we have sweated all day in the blazing sun." The owner turned to one of them, and said: "My friend, I am not being unfair to you. Did we not agree on one silver coin? Take your wage and go home. I choose to pay the last men the same as you. Surely I am free to do what I like with my own money. Why be jealous because I am generous?"

'Thus the last will be first, and the first will be last.'

Matthew 20. 1–6a, 8–16

True simplicity

Jesus exclaimed: 'I thank you, Father, Lord of heaven and earth, for hiding these things from the wise and the learned, and revealing them to those who are simple. Yes, Father, such was your choice. Everything has been entrusted to me by my Father. And no one knows the Son except the Father; just as no one knows the Father except the Son, and those to whom the Son chooses to reveal him.

'Come to me, all who are weary and whose load is heavy, and I shall give you rest. Take my yoke upon you and learn from me, for I am gentle and humble in heart, and you will find rest for your souls. My yoke is easy and my load is light.'

One sabbath at around this time Jesus was walking through cornfields. His disciples were hungry, and began to pick ears of corn and eat them. The Pharisees saw this, and said to him: 'Look, your disciples are doing what is forbidden on the sabbath.' He answered: 'The Son of Man is master of the sabbath.'

Matthew 11.25—12.2, 8

The greatest commandment

One of the teachers of the law, who had heard these discussions and had observed how well Jesus answered, came forward and asked a further question: 'Which is the first of all the commandments?' Jesus replied: 'The first is this: "Listen, Israel, the Lord our God is the one Lord, and you must love the Lord your God with all your heart, with all your soul, with all your mind and with all your strength." The second is this: "You must love your neighbour as yourself." There is no commandment greater than these.'

The teacher of the law said to him: 'Well spoken, Master. You are right to say that God is one and beside him there is no other. And to love him with all your heart, all your mind and all your strength, and to love your neighbour as yourself, is far more important than offering animals and other sacrifices to God.' When Jesus heard how wisely he spoke, he said: 'You are not far from the kingdom of God.' After this no one dared to ask Jesus any more questions.

Mark 12.28–34

Resolving conflict

Jesus instructed his disciples: 'If your brother does wrong, go and take the matter up with him alone. If he listens to you, then you have won your brother back. But if he will not listen, take one or two others with you, so that the case may be settled on the testimony of two or three witnesses. If he refuses to listen to them, report the matter to the congregation; and if he will not listen to the full congregation, treat him as though he were a pagan or a tax collector.

'So in truth I tell you: whatever you forbid on earth, shall be forbidden in heaven; and whatever you permit on earth, will be permitted in heaven.

'And I tell you once again, if two of you on earth agree about any request you make, that request will be granted by my heavenly Father. For where two or three gather in my name, I am there among them.'

Matthew 18.15–20

The lost sheep and lost coin

Tax collectors and sinners crowded round Jesus to listen to him. The Pharisees and teachers of the law began murmuring their disapproval, saying: 'This man welcomes sinners and eats with them.'

Jesus answered them in parables: 'If you have a hundred sheep and lose one of them, what do you do? You leave the other ninety-nine sheep in the pasture, and go after the one that is missing until you find it. And when you do, you joyfully lift it on your shoulders and carry it back home. Then you call your friends and neighbours together, saying to them: "Rejoice with me, I have found my lost sheep." In the same way, I tell you, there will be more joy in heaven over one sinner who repents, than over ninety-nine righteous people who have no need of repentance.

'Or again, if a woman has ten silver coins and loses one of them, what does she do? She lights a lamp, sweeps out the house, and searches everywhere until she finds it. And when she does, she calls her friends and neighbours together, saying to them: "Rejoice with me. I have found the coin that I lost." In the same way, I tell you, there is joy among the angels of God over one repentant sinner.'

Luke 15.1–10

The lost son

Jesus gave this further parable: 'A man had two sons. The younger son said to him: "Father, give me my share of the property now." So he divided his estate between them. A few days later the younger son turned the whole of his share into cash, and left for a distant country where he squandered it on corrupt pleasures.

'When he had spent it all, a severe famine spread over that country, and he found himself in need. So he hired himself out to a local landowner, who sent him to take care of his pigs. He would willingly have filled himself with the husks the pigs were eating, but no one gave him anything. A last he came to his senses, saying to himself: "My father's servants have all the food they want, while I am here starving to death! I shall go at once to my father, and confess to him that I have sinned against God and against him. I am no longer fit to be called his son; I shall ask to be treated as a hired servant."

'So he set out for his father's house. While he was still a long way off, his father saw him, and his heart went out to him. He ran to meet his son, threw his arms round him, and kissed him. "Father," the son said, "I have sinned against God and against you. I am no longer fit to be called your son." But the father called his servants, and said: "Hurry, fetch the best robe and put it on him; put a ring on his finger and sandals on his feet. Bring the fatted calf and kill it, and we shall celebrate with a feast. For this son of mine was dead and has come back to life; he was lost and is found." And they began to celebrate.'

Luke 15.11–24

The elder son

Jesus continued: 'The elder son had been out on the farm. On his way back, as he approached the house, he heard music and dancing. He called one of the servants and asked what was happening. The servant replied: "Your brother has returned home, and your father has killed the fatted calf because he has got him back safe and sound." The elder son was angry and refused to go in. His father came out and pleaded with him. But he retorted: "All these years I have slaved for you, never disobeying your orders; yet you never offered me so much as a goat, to celebrate with my friends. Now that this son of yours appears, having wasted all your money on prostitutes, you kill the fatted calf for him." "My boy," said the father, "you are always with me, and everything I have is yours. Surely we had to celebrate this happy day. Your brother was dead, and is now alive; he was lost and has been found."'

Luke 15.25–32

The Pharisee and the tax collector

Jesus told this parable to people who took pride in their own goodness and despised everyone else: 'Two men went up to the temple to pray, one a Pharisee and the other a tax collector. The Pharisee stood up and prayed: "I thank you, God, that I am not greedy, dishonest or adulterous like everyone else, and especially that I am not like this tax collector here. I fast twice a week, and I give you a tenth of all my income."

'The tax collector stood apart and would not even raise his eyes to heaven. He beat his breast and cried: "God, have mercy on me, a sinner!" '

Jesus concluded: 'It was the tax collector, I tell you, and not the Pharisee, who went home acquitted of his sins. For those who exalt themselves will be humbled; and those who humble themselves will be exalted.'

Luke 18.9–14

True greatness

They came to Capernaum. And when they had gone indoors, Jesus asked his disciples: 'What were you arguing about on the road?' They were silent, because on the way they had been discussing which of them was the greatest. So Jesus sat down, called the twelve disciples to him, and declared: 'Those who want to be first, must make themselves last of all and servant of all.' Then he took a child, and set him in front of them. Putting his arm round the child, he said to the disciples: 'Whoever welcomes a little child such as this in my name, welcomes me; and whoever welcomes me, welcomes not me but the one who sent me.'

John said to him: 'Master, we saw someone driving out demons in your name; and, as he was not one of us, we tried to stop him.' Jesus said: 'Do not stop him; no one who performs a miracle in my name will be able the next moment to speak evil of me. He who is not against us, is for us. In truth I tell you, whoever gives you a cup of water to drink because you are followers of the Christ, will certainly not go unrewarded. But if anyone causes the downfall of one of these little ones who have faith, it would be better for him to be thrown into the sea with a millstone round his neck.'

Mark 9.33–42

Peter's declaration

When Jesus came to the region of Caesarea Philippi, he asked his disciples: 'Who do people say that the Son of Man is?' They replied: 'Some say John the Baptist, some Elijah, others Jeremiah or one of the prophets.' Jesus asked: 'And who do you say that I am?' Simon Peter answered: 'You are the Christ, the Son of the living God.' 'Simon, son of Jonah,' Jesus said, 'you are truly blessed. You did not learn this from any human being; it was revealed to you by my heavenly Father. So I say, you are Peter, the rock; on this rock I shall build my church, and the power of death will never over-power it. I shall give you the keys of the kingdom of heaven. Whatever you forbid on earth, shall be forbidden in heaven; and whatever you permit on earth, shall be permitted in heaven.' He then gave his disciples strict orders not to tell anyone that he was the Christ.

From that time Jesus began to make it clear to his disciples that he had to go to Jerusalem, where he would suffer griev-ously at the hands of the elders, chief priests and teachers of the law, be put to death, and be raised up on the third day. At this Peter took hold of him and began to rebuke him: 'Heaven preserve you, Lord, this will never happen to you.' Jesus turned to Peter, and replied: 'Get behind me, Satan, you are an obstacle on my path. You think as humans think, not as God thinks.'

Matthew 16.13–23

The transfiguration

About a week later Jesus took Peter, John and James, and went up a mountain to pray. And, while he was praying, the appearance of his face changed, and his clothes became dazzling white. Suddenly two men were talking with him; they were Moses and Elijah, in heavenly glory. They spoke of how Jesus would soon fulfil God's purpose through dying in Jerusalem. Peter and his companions had been overcome by sleep but, when they woke up, they saw the glory of Jesus and two men standing with him. As the two men were leaving Jesus, Peter said to him: 'Master, it is good that we are here. Shall we make three shelters, one for you, one for Moses and one for Elijah?' He did not know what he was saying. As he spoke a cloud came and cast its shadow over them; and as the cloud covered them the disciples were afraid. From the cloud a voice was heard: 'This is my Son, whom I have chosen; listen to him.' After the voice had spoken, Jesus was alone. The disciples kept quiet about these events, telling no one at that time what they had seen.

Luke 9.28–36

The unforgiving debtor

Peter came to Jesus, and asked: 'Lord, how often must I forgive my brother if he continues to wrong me? As many as seven times?' Jesus replied: 'Not seven, I say to you, but seventy times seven.

'The kingdom of heaven can be compared with a king who decided to settle accounts with the men who served him. At the outset a man was brought to him who owed ten thousand gold coins. Since this servant had no means of paying, his master ordered him to be sold as a slave, together with his wife and children and all he possessed, to meet the debt. The servant fell at his master's feet, and cried: "Be patient with me, and I shall pay you in full." The king felt so sorry for him that he let the servant go, and cancelled the debt.

'As the servant went out, he met a fellow servant who owed him only a few gold coins. He seized him by the throat, and demanded that he repay his debt. His fellow servant fell at his feet, and cried: "Be patient with me, and I shall repay you." But he refused, and had him thrown into prison until he could pay the debt. When they saw what had happened, the other servants were deeply distressed, and they went to their master to report the affair. The master sent for the man, and said: "You scoundrel! I cancelled the whole of your debt when you appealed to me. Were you not bound to show mercy to your fellow servant as I showed mercy to you?" And in his anger the master condemned the man to be tortured until he should pay the debt in full.'

Matthew 18.21–34

The gold coins

Jesus related this parable: 'A man of noble birth was going away for a time, to be appointed king in a distant country. Before leaving he gave to each of his servants a gold coin, saying: "Trade with these while I am away."

'When he returned, he called the servants to find out what profit each had made. The first came and said: "Sir, I have earned ten gold coins with the one you gave me." The king replied: "Well done; you are a good servant. Since you have proved trustworthy in a small matter, I shall put you in charge of ten cities." The second came and said: "Sir, I have earned five gold coins with the one you gave me." "You shall be in charge of five cities," the king said.

'The third came and said: "Sir, here is your gold coin wrapped up in a handkerchief. I was afraid of you, because you are a hard man. You take what you do not own, and you reap what you did not sow." The king cried: "You scoundrel! I shall condemn you out of your own mouth. You knew me to be a hard man, taking what I do not own, and reaping what I have not sown. Then why did you not put my money in the bank, so that I could have drawn out interest on my return?" And he said to those standing by: "Take the gold coin from him, and give it to the man with the most." "But, sir," they replied, "he already has ten gold coins." The king concluded: "I tell you: those who have something will be given more; but those who have nothing will forfeit even what they have."'

Luke 19.12–13, 15–26

True service

Jesus and his disciples were on the road going up to Jerusalem, with Jesus leading the way.

James and John, the sons of Zebedee, approached him, and said: 'Master, we want you to do us a favour.' 'What do you want me to do for you?' Jesus asked. They replied: 'Allow us to sit with you in your glory, with one of us on your right hand and the other on your left.' Jesus said: 'You do not understand what you are asking. Can you drink the cup that I drink, and be baptized in the way I must be baptized?' 'We can,' they answered. Jesus said to them: 'You will indeed drink the cup I shall drink, and be baptized in the way I must be baptized. But as for seats on my right or my left, these are not mine to grant; that honour is for those to whom they have already been assigned.'

When the other ten heard about this request, they were indignant with James and John. Jesus called them to him, and said: 'You know that in the world the recognized rulers lord it over their subjects, and the great men assert their authority. Among you this shall not be so. Those who want to be great, must be servants to the rest; and those who want to be first, must be slaves to all. For the Son of Man did not come to be served but to serve, and to give his life as a ransom for many.'

Mark 10.32a, 35–45

The resurrection and the life

A man named Lazarus fell ill. His home was in Bethany, where his sisters Mary and Martha also lived. The sisters sent a message to Jesus: 'Lord, your dear friend is ill.'

When Jesus arrived, he found that Lazarus had already been four days in the tomb. When Martha heard that Jesus was coming, she went to meet him; Mary remained sitting in the house. 'Lord,' Martha said to Jesus, 'if you had been here, my brother would not have died. But even now I know that God will grant whatever you ask of him.' 'Your brother will rise again,' Jesus said. She replied: 'I know that he will rise to life on the last day.' Jesus said to her: 'I am the resurrection and the life. Those who believe in me, though they die, will live; and those who live and believe in me, will never die. Do you believe this?' She answered: 'I do, Lord; I believe that you are the Christ, the Son of God who was to come into the world.'

When Martha had made this declaration, she went to call her sister Mary. Taking her aside she said: 'The Master is here and is asking for you.' At once Mary rose up and went out to see him. Jesus had not yet entered the village, but was still at the place where Martha had met him. The people, who had been in the house comforting Mary, followed her when she hurried out. They assumed she was going to the tomb to weep there.

John 11.1, 3, 17–31

The raising of Lazarus

Mary went to Jesus; and as soon as she saw him, she threw herself at his feet. 'Lord, if you had been here, my brother would not have died.' When Jesus saw that she was weeping, and that the people with her were also weeping, he sighed heavily and was deeply moved. 'Where have you laid him?' Jesus asked. 'Come and see,' they replied. Jesus wept. And the people said: 'See how dearly he must have loved him.' But some remarked: 'He opened a blind man's eyes; surely he could have prevented Lazarus from dying.'

Jesus, again sighing deeply, went to the tomb, which was a cave with a stone placed at the entrance. 'Take the stone away,' Jesus ordered. 'Lord,' said Martha, the dead man's sister, 'by now there will be a stench; he has been there four days.' Jesus said: 'Have I not told you that, if you have faith, you will see the glory of God?' So they moved the stone away.

Jesus looked upwards, and said: 'Father, I thank you for hearing my prayer. I know that you always hear me; but I speak for the sake of those standing around me, that they may believe you who sent me.' Then he raised his voice: 'Lazarus, come out!' The dead man came out, his hands and feet bound with linen bandages, and his face covered with a cloth. Jesus said: 'Untie him, and let him go.'

John 11.32–44

The start of the plot

Many of the people who had come to visit Mary, and had
seen what Jesus did, believed in him. But some went off to
the Pharisees, and reported what he had done. So the chief
priests and the Pharisees called a meeting, and said to one another: 'What shall we do? This man is performing many
signs. If we let him go on like this, everybody will believe in
him; and the Romans will come and sweep away our temple
and our nation.' But one of the them, Caiaphas, who was
high priest that year, said: 'You have not grasped the situation
at all; you do not realize where your advantage lies. It is better
that one man should die for the people, rather than the whole
nation be destroyed.' He did not say this of his own accord;
but as the high priest that year he was prophesying that Jesus
would die for the Jewish people – and not only for them, but
also to gather together all the scattered children of God.

So from that day onwards they plotted his death.

John 11.45–53

The anointing at Bethany

Six days before the Passover festival Jesus went to Bethany, the home of Lazarus whom he had raised from the dead. A supper was given in his honour; Martha waited at table and Lazarus was among the guests sitting with Jesus. Then Mary brought in a pound of very costly perfume, pure oil of nard; and with it she anointed Jesus's feet, and wiped them with her hair. The whole house was filled with the fragrance. At this one of Jesus's disciples, Judas Iscariot, who was to betray him, protested: 'Why was this perfume not sold for three hundred silver coins, and the money given to the poor?' He said this, not out of concern for the poor, but because he was a thief; he had charge of the common purse, and used to pilfer money kept in it. Jesus said: 'Leave her alone; let her keep it for the day of my burial. The poor you have always with you; but you will not always have me.'

Meanwhile a large number of people heard that Jesus was in Bethany; and many came there, not only because of Jesus, but also to see Lazarus whom he had raised from the dead. The chief priests then resolved to do away with Lazarus as well, since on his account many people were rejecting them and putting their faith in Jesus.

John 12.1–11

Entry into Jerusalem

Jesus and his disciples were now approaching Jerusalem; and when they reached Bethphage at the Mount of Olives, Jesus sent off two of his disciples, saying: 'Go to the village ahead of you, and there you will at once find a tethered donkey with her foal beside her. Untie them, and bring them to me. If anyone says anything to you, answer, "The Master needs them," and he will let you have them immediately.'

The disciples went and did as Jesus had directed, bringing the donkey and her foal. They laid cloaks on the donkey's back, and Jesus mounted. Crowds of people spread their cloaks on the road, and some cut branches from trees to spread in his path. The people walking in front of Jesus and those following shouted out: 'Hosanna to the Son of David! Blessed is he who comes in the name of the Lord! Hosanna in the highest heavens!'

When Jesus entered Jerusalem the whole city went wild with excitement. 'Who is this?' people asked. And the crowds replied: 'This is the prophet Jesus from Nazareth in Galilee.'

Matthew 21.1−3, 6−11

Entry into the temple

Jesus went into the temple, and drove out all who were buying and selling in the temple precincts. He overturned the tables of the money changers and the seats of those who sold pigeons, saying to them: 'Scripture says, "My house shall be called a house of prayer," but you are making it a den of thieves.'

The blind and the crippled came to him in the temple, and he healed them. The chief priests and teachers of the law became angry as they watched the wonderful things he was doing, and heard the children in the temple shouting: 'Hosanna to the Son of David.' They asked Jesus: 'Do you hear what they are saying?' Jesus replied: 'I do. Have you never read the text, "Your praises are on the lips even of children and babies"?' Then he left and went out to the city of Bethany, where he spent the night.

Matthew 21.12–17

To Caesar and to God

The teachers of the law and chief priests awaited their opportunity, and sent agents in the guise of honest men. Their task was to trap Jesus into saying something that could be used as a pretext for handing him over to the jurisdiction and power of the Roman governor. 'Master,' these agents said, 'we know that what you speak and teach is right; you show favour to no one, but teach in all sincerity the way of God. Is it against our law to pay taxes to the Roman emperor, or not?'

Jesus saw through their trick. So he said to them: 'Show me a silver coin. Whose head does it bear, and whose inscription?' 'Caesar's,' they replied. 'Very well then,' Jesus concluded, 'pay to Caesar what belongs to Caesar, and pay to God what belongs to God.'

They were astonished at his answer, and fell silent. Thus their attempt to catch him out in public failed.

Luke 20.20–26

The widow's gift

Jesus sat down opposite the temple treasury, and watched the people dropping in their money. Many of the rich put in large sums. A poor widow arrived and dropped in two small copper coins. Jesus called his disciples to him, and said: 'In truth I tell you, this poor widow has put in more money than all the rest. They have more than enough money, and gave what they could spare. But she, with less than enough, gave all that she had to live on.'

As Jesus was leaving the temple, one of his disciples exclaimed: 'Look, Master, at those huge stones and fine buildings.' Jesus said: 'Do you see these great buildings? Not a single stone will be left on another; they will all be thrown down.'

Mark 12.41—13.2

The final judgement

Jesus said to his disciples: 'When the Son of Man comes as king, he will sit on his royal throne, with the people of all nations assembled before him. He will divide them into two groups – as the shepherd separates the sheep from the goats, placing the sheep on his right hand and the goats on his left. Then the king will say to those on his right: "You have the Father's blessing; come and take possession of the kingdom which was prepared for you at the creation of the world. For when I was hungry, you gave me food; when I was thirsty, you gave me drink; when I was a stranger, you took me into your home; when I was naked, you clothed me; when I was sick, you came to my aid; when I was in prison, you visited me." The righteous will answer him: "Lord, when did we do these things for you?" And the king will say: 'When you did these things for even the least important of these brothers of mine, you did them for me."

'Then the king will say to those on his left: "You are under a curse; go from my sight to the eternal fire that the devil and his angels have prepared for you. For when I was hungry, you gave me nothing to eat; when thirsty, nothing to drink; when I was a stranger, you did not welcome me; when naked, you did not clothe me; when I was ill and in prison, you did not help me." And they will reply: "Lord, when did we see you hungry, thirsty, a stranger, naked, ill or in prison, and do nothing for you?" And the king will say: "In truth I tell you, when you failed to do such things for even the least of these brothers of mine, you failed to do them for me."'

Matthew 25.31–45

The upper room

It was now two days before the festival of Passover. The chief priests and teachers of the law were trying to devise a scheme to arrest Jesus and put him to death. They said: 'It must not be during the festival, or the people will riot.'

Judas Iscariot, one of the twelve disciples, approached the chief priests offering to betray Jesus to them. They were delighted with his proposal, and promised to give him money; and he began to look for an opportunity to hand Jesus over to them.

On the first day of the festival, when the Passover lambs were being slaughtered, his disciples asked him: 'Where do you want us to go and prepare the Passover meal for you?' Jesus chose two disciples, and instructed them: 'Go into the city, where you will meet a man carrying a pitcher of water. Follow him, and when he enters a house, say to the owner: "The Master asks where is the room in which he and his disciples will eat the Passover meal?" He will show you a large upper room, with couches already set out. Make the preparations for us there.'

The disciples went off to the city, and found everything just as Jesus had told them; and they prepared the Passover meal.

Mark 14.1–2, 10–16

The last supper

When the time came, Jesus and the apostles took their places at table. He said to them: 'I have longed to eat this Passover meal with you before my death. For I tell you, I shall not eat it again until it is fulfilled in the kingdom of God.'

Then he took bread, offered thanks, broke it, and gave it to them, saying: 'This is my body, given for you; do this in memory of me.' In the same way he gave them the cup after supper, saying: 'This cup is the new covenant sealed with my blood, which is poured out for you.'

Jesus added: 'Even now the hand of my betrayer is with me at this table. The Son of Man is on the path which has been decreed; but how terrible it will be for the man who betrays him.' The disciples began to ask one another which of them could possibly do this.

Then a dispute arose about which of them should be considered greatest. But Jesus said: 'Who is greater: he who sits at table or the one who serves him? Surely the one who sits at table. Yet I am among you as a servant.'

Luke 22.14–16, 19–24, 27

The washing of feet

Now Jesus rose from table, took off his outer garment and tied a towel round his waist. Then he poured water into a basin, and began to wash his disciples' feet, wiping them with the towel. He came to Simon Peter, who said to him: 'You, Lord, washing my feet?' Jesus answered: 'At present you do not understand what I am doing, but one day you will.' 'Then, Lord,' said Simon Peter, 'do not wash only my feet; wash my hands and head as well!' Jesus said: 'Those who have had a bath are completely clean and need no further washing. All of you are clean, all of you except one.' He added the words 'except one' because he knew who was going to betray him.

After washing their feet, he put on his outer garment. Then he sat down again, and spoke to them: 'Do you understand what I have done for you? You call me Master and Lord, and rightly so, because that is what I am. If I, then, your Lord and Master, have washed your feet, you also ought to wash one another's feet. I have set you an example: you are to do as I have done for you. In all truth I tell you, no servant is greater than his master, and no messenger is greater than the one who sent him. Now that you know this, blessed are you if you act upon it.'

John 13.4–17

The gift of peace

Jesus continued: 'If you love me, you will keep my commands. I shall ask the Father, and he will give you another counsellor, who will be with you forever, the Spirit of truth. The world cannot accept him, since it neither sees nor knows him; but you know him, because he is with you, and is in you. I shall not leave you bereft; I am coming back to you. In a little while the world will see me no more, but you will see me; and because I live, you also will live. On that day you will know that I am in my Father, and you are in me, and I am in you.

'Those who love me, obey my teaching, and my Father will love them; we shall come to them, and live within them. But those who do not love me, do not obey my teaching. And the teaching which you have heard, is not my own; it comes from the Father, who sent me.

'I have told you these things while I am still with you. But the counsellor, the Holy Spirit whom the Father will send in my name, will teach you everything, and remind you of all that I have told you.

'Peace I leave you; my own peace I give you, such as the world cannot give. Set your troubled hearts at rest, and banish your fears.'

John 14.15–20, 23–27

The true vine

'I am the true vine, and my Father is the gardener. Every branch of mine that does not bear fruit, he cuts away; and every branch that does bear fruit, he prunes, to make it clean and bear even more fruit. You have already been made clean by the teaching I have given you. Dwell in me, as I dwell in you. A branch cannot bear fruit by itself, but can only bear fruit if it is united with the vine. In the same way you cannot bear fruit unless you are united with me.

'I am the vine and you are the branches. Those who dwell in me, and I in them, bear much fruit; apart from me you can do nothing. Those who do not dwell in me are thrown away like withered branches; then they are gathered up, thrown in the fire and burnt.

'I have spoken in this way to you, so that my joy may be in you, and your joy may be complete. This is my command: love one another, as I have loved you. There is no love greater than this, that a man lays down his life for his friends. You are my friends, if you do what I command you. No longer do I call you servants, because servants do not know what their master is doing. Instead I call you friends, because I have made known to you everything I have learnt from my Father. You did not choose me; I chose you. I appointed you to go and bear fruit, the kind of fruit that will last, so that the Father will give you everything you ask in my name. This is my command to you: love one another.'

John 15.1–6, 11–17

The anguish of Jesus

Jesus now went with his disciples to a place called Geth-semane, and said to them: 'Sit down while I go over there to pray.' He took Peter and the two sons of Zebedee with him. Grief and anguish overwhelmed him, and he said: 'My heart is almost breaking with sorrow. Wait here and stay awake with me.' Then he went a little further, and threw himself down, praying: 'My Father, if it is possible, let this cup pass me by. Yet not my will, but yours, be done.'

He returned to the three disciples, and found them asleep. He cried out: 'Could none of you stay awake with me even for one hour? Keep watch, and pray that you may be spared the test. The spirit is willing, but the flesh is weak.'

He went away a second time, and prayed: 'My Father, if this cup cannot pass me by, but I must drink it, let your will be done.' He returned once more to the disciples; but their eyes were so heavy that they were asleep.

Again Jesus left them, and went away to pray for the third time, saying the same words. Then he returned to the dis-ciples, and said to them: 'Are you still sleeping and resting? The hour has come. The Son of Man is to be betrayed into the hands of sinners. Get up and let us go. The traitor is near.'

Matthew 26.36–46

The arrest of Jesus

While Jesus was still speaking, a large crowd appeared; they were armed with swords and cudgels, and had been sent by the chief priests and elders of the nation. Judas had arranged a sign with the crowd: 'The one I kiss is the man you want; arrest him.' Judas went straight up to Jesus, and said, 'Peace be with you, Master.' Then he kissed him. 'My friend,' Jesus replied, 'do what you have to do.' The crowd came forward, seized Jesus and held him tight.

One of those with Jesus reached for his sword and drew it; he struck the high priest's servant, cutting off his ear. Jesus said: 'Put away your sword; all who live by the sword, die by the sword. Do you suppose that I cannot appeal for help to my Father, who would at once send more than twelve legions of angels? But how then would the scriptures be fulfilled which say that this must happen?'

Jesus turned to the crowd, and said: 'Do you take me for a bandit, that you have to come out with swords and cudgels to arrest me? Day after day I sat teaching in the temple, but you did not lay hands on me. But this has happened to fulfil the words of the prophets.'

Then all the disciples deserted him and ran away.

Matthew 26.47–56

Jesus before the Jewish Council

The men who had arrested Jesus led him off to the house of
Caiaphas the high priest, where the teachers of the law and
elders had gathered. They were looking for some allegation
against Jesus that would warrant a death sentence; but, although many came forward with lies, they found no firm
evidence. Finally two men came forward, claiming Jesus had
said, 'I can tear down God's temple, and rebuild it in three
days'. The high priest rose and said to Jesus: 'Have you no
answer to the accusations that these witnesses are bringing
against you?' But Jesus remained silent. The high priest then
cried: 'By the living God I demand that you tell us: are you
the Christ, the Son of God?'

Jesus replied: 'The words are yours. But I tell you that
from this time onward you will see the Son of Man seated at
the right hand of the Almighty and coming on clouds of
heaven.' At this the high priest tore his robes, and exclaimed:
'This is blasphemy; we need no further witnesses. You have
just heard the blasphemy. What is your verdict?' They answered: 'He is guilty; he must die.'

Then they spat in his face and beat him with their fists.
And as they hit him, some said: 'Now, Christ, if you are a
prophet, tell us who hit you.'

                                         Matthew 26.57, 59–68

The death of Judas

When Judas the traitor learnt that Jesus had been condemned, he was filled with remorse. He went to the chief priests and elders with the money they had paid him; it was thirty pieces of silver. He exclaimed: 'I have sinned; I have betrayed an innocent man.' But they said: 'What is that to us? It is your concern.' So Judas flung the money on the ground, and left. Then he went off, and hanged himself.

The chief priests picked up the coins, saying: 'This is blood money, so it cannot be put into the temple treasury.' After discussing the matter, they used the money to buy the potter's field as a cemetery for foreigners. That is why the piece of land is still called the Field of Blood.

Matthew 27.3–8

Jesus before Pilate

Early in the morning Jesus was taken from the house of Caiaphas to the governor's palace, since at the time of the Passover they wished to avoid being defiled. Pilate came out to see them, and asked them: 'What charge do you bring against this man?' They replied: 'If he were not a criminal, we should not have brought him before you.' Pilate said: 'Take him yourselves, and try him by your own laws.' 'We are not allowed to put anyone to death,' they answered.

Pilate went back into his palace and summoned Jesus. 'Are you the king of the Jews?' he asked. Jesus said: 'Does this question come from you, or have others suggested it to you?' Pilate said: 'Do you think I am a Jew? Your own people and their chief priest have brought you before me. What have you done?' Jesus replied: 'My kingdom does not belong to this world; if it did, my followers would have fought to prevent my arrest by the Jewish authorities. My kingdom belongs elsewhere.' 'So are you a king?' Pilate asked. Jesus said: 'It is you who uses the word "king". My task is to bear witness to the truth. For this purpose I was born and I came into the world. And all who are not deaf to the truth, listen to my voice.' 'What is truth?' Pilate said.

With these words Pilate went out again to the people, and pronounced: 'I can find no case against him.'

John 18.28–38

The condemnation of Jesus

At every Passover festival it was the Roman governor's custom to release one prisoner chosen by the people. A notorious criminal called Jesus Barabbas was in custody at this time. When the people gathered, Pilate asked them: 'Which one do you want me to release, Jesus Barabbas or Jesus called the Christ?' He knew that the Jewish authorities had handed Jesus over to him out of malice.

When Pilate was sitting in the chair of judgement, a message came to him from his wife, which ran: 'Have nothing to do with that innocent man; I was much troubled in my dreams last night on his account.'

Meanwhile the chief priests and elders had persuaded the crowd to demand the release of Barabbas and the execution of Jesus. So when the governor asked, 'Which of these two do you want me to release?' The crowd answered: 'Barabbas!' 'In that case, what am I to do with Jesus called the Christ?' Pilate asked. With one voice they cried: 'Crucify him!' 'But what harm has he done?' Pilate asked. But they shouted even louder: 'Crucify him!'

Pilate saw that he was making no impression, and that a riot might break out. So he took some water and washed his hands in full view of the people, declaring: 'I am clean of this man's blood; it is your concern.' The whole crowd answered: 'Let his blood be on us and our children.' Then Pilate released Barabbas for them. And after having Jesus flogged, he handed him over to be crucified.

Matthew 27.15–26

The crown of thorns

Pilate's soldiers took hold of Jesus, and a whole cohort collected round him. They stripped him and dressed him in a scarlet cloak; they twisted some thorns into a crown and placed it on his head; and they put a reed in his right hand. Then they fell on their knees and jeered at him. 'Hail, king of the Jews!' they cried. After that they spat at him. Finally they took the stick from his hand, and beat him about the head with it. When they had finished mocking him, they stripped off the cloak, and dressed him again in his own clothes.

Matthew 27.27–31*a*

The crucifixion of Jesus

The soldiers now led Jesus away to execution. As they were going they seized a man called Simon from Cyrene, who was coming in from the country; they put the cross on his back, and made him carry it behind Jesus.

A large crowd followed him, including many women who wept and wailed for him. Jesus turned to them, and said: 'Daughters of Jerusalem, do not weep for me; weep for yourselves and your children. The days are coming when people will say: "Blessed are those who are barren, the wombs that never bore a child, the breasts that never fed one." Then they will say to the mountains, "Fall on us," and to the hills, "Hide us." For if these things are done when the wood is green, what will happen when it is dry?'

Two other men were led out to be executed with Jesus; they were both criminals. When they reached the place called 'The Skull', the soldiers crucified Jesus, and also the two criminals, one on his right and the other on his left. Jesus said: 'Father, forgive them; they do not know what they are doing.' The soldiers shared out his clothes by casting lots.

Luke 23.26–34

The mocking of Jesus

The people stood watching. Their leaders taunted Jesus, crying: 'He saved others; now, if he is the Christ of God, the chosen one, let him save himself.' The soldiers joined in the mockery, exclaiming: 'If you are king of the Jews, save yourself.' Above him was an inscription: 'This is the king of the Jews.'

One of the criminals hanging there jeered at Jesus: 'Are you not the Christ? Then save yourself and us.' But the other criminal rebuked him, shouting back: 'Have you no fear of God? You received the same sentence as he did. But we are paying the price for our crimes, while this man has done nothing wrong.' And he said to Jesus: 'Remember me, Jesus, when you come as king.' Jesus replied: 'In truth I tell you, today you will be with me in paradise.'

Luke 23.35–36a, 37–43

The agony of Jesus

At noon darkness fell over the whole land. It lasted for three hours. Then Jesus cried out: 'Eli, Eli, lema sabachthani?' – which means: 'My God, my God, why have you forsaken me?' Hearing these words some of the people standing there said: 'He is calling Elijah'. One of them ran at once to fetch a sponge; he soaked it in sour wine and held it on a stick to the lips of Jesus. Others said: 'Let us see if Elijah will come and save him.'

Matthew 27.45–49

The death of Jesus

The curtain of the temple was torn into two. Jesus gave out a loud cry: 'Father, into your hands I commit my spirit.' And with these words he died.

When the centurion standing by saw what had happened, he praised God and said: 'Truly, this was a good man.' The crowd who had gathered for the spectacle, when they saw what had happened, went home beating their breasts.

Luke 23.45b–48

The burial of Jesus

Joseph of Arimathaea, a disciple of Jesus who had kept his allegiance secret for fear of the Jewish authorities, asked Pilate to let him remove the body of Jesus. Pilate consented, so Joseph came and took the body. Nicodemus, the man who had visited Jesus at night, accompanied Joseph, bringing with him a mixture of myrrh and aloes. Following the Jewish custom, they wrapped the body, along with the spices, in strips of linen cloth.

Near the place where Jesus had been crucified was a garden; and in the garden was a new tomb in which no one had yet been buried. Since it was the eve of the sabbath and the tomb was close by, Joseph and Nicodemus laid Jesus there.

John 19.38–42

The empty tomb

Early on the first day of the week, while it was still dark, Mary of Magdala came to the tomb. She saw that the stone had been moved from the entrance. So she ran to Simon Peter and the other disciple whom Jesus loved, and said: 'They have taken the Lord out of the tomb, and we do not know where they have put him.'

Peter set out with the other disciple to the tomb. Both were running, but the other disciple, running faster than Peter, reached the tomb first. He peered in and saw the strips of linen cloth lying there; but he did not enter. Simon Peter caught up with him, and went into the tomb. He saw the linen strips on the ground, and also the cloth that had been round his head; it was not with the strips, but was rolled up by itself. Then the disciple who had arrived first at the tomb, also went in. He saw and he believed.

John 20. 1–8

The appearance at the tomb

Mary of Magdala stood outside the tomb weeping. As she wept, she peered into the tomb, and saw two angels in white sitting where the body of Jesus had been, one at the head and the other at the feet. 'Woman,' they asked her, 'why are you weeping?' She replied: 'They have taken my Lord away, and I do not know where they have put him.'

Then she turned round and saw Jesus standing there; but she did not recognize him. Jesus asked her: 'Why are you weeping? Who are you looking for?' Thinking that he was the gardener, she said: 'If it is you who removed him, sir, tell me where you have laid him, and I shall take him away.' Jesus said to her, 'Mary!' She looked up at him, and said, 'Rabboni!' which is Hebrew for 'Master'. Jesus said: 'Do not cling to me, because I have not yet ascended to my Father and your Father, my God and your God.'

John 20. 11–17

The appearances in the locked room

The disciples kept the doors locked, for fear of the Jewish authorities. But late that evening Jesus appeared and stood among them. 'Peace be with you,' he said to them; and he showed them his hands and his side. The disciples were filled with joy at seeing the Lord. Jesus again said, 'Peace be with you'. And he added: 'As the Father sent me, so I send you'. Then he breathed on them, saying: 'Receive the Holy Spirit. If you forgive anyone's sins, they are forgiven; if you do not forgive them, they remain unforgiven.'

One of the twelve disciples, Thomas called the Twin, was not with the others when Jesus came. They kept telling him: 'We have seen the Lord'. But he replied: 'Unless I see the marks of the nails on his hands, and can put my finger into the holes which the nails made, and unless I can put my hand into his side, I shall not believe.'

A week later the disciples were gathered in the same room, and Thomas was with them. Although the doors were locked, Jesus came and stood among them. 'Peace be with you,' he said. Then he turned to Thomas, and said: 'Put your finger here, and look at my hands. Stretch out your hand and put it in my side. Stop your doubting and believe!' 'My Lord and my God,' Thomas exclaimed. Jesus said: 'You believe because you can see me; blessed are those who believe without seeing me.'

John 20. 19–29

The mission to the world

Jesus told the eleven disciples to go up a hill to Galilee, and he appeared to them there. When they saw him they fell on their knees, although some still had doubts. Jesus came near to them, and said: 'Full authority in heaven and on earth has been given to me. Go, therefore, to all peoples everywhere and make them my disciples. Baptize them in the name of the Father, the Son and the Holy Spirit; and teach them to obey all the commands I gave you. I shall be with you always, to the end of time.'

Matthew 28.16–20

THE EARLY CHURCH

When Luke wrote his gospel, he added a second book in which he relates the activities of the first Christians. In Luke's understanding Jesus ascended to heaven, and then sent his Spirit to the disciples; and the book opens with these episodes. He then describes the common life of the first Christian community, followed by an account of the death of Stephen, the first Christian martyr. Thereafter the focus of the book is the personality and work of Paul: his conversion from being a persecutor of Christians to being the most ardent advocate of the Christian faith; his efforts to spread Christianity beyond the confines of Judaism; the conference in Jerusalem which these efforts provoked; and his own arrest and trial, finishing with his arrival at Rome to appear before the emperor.

The ascension of Jesus

Over a period of forty days after his death Jesus appeared many times to his disciples, giving ample proof that he was alive; and he spoke to them about the kingdom of God. While he was with them, he instructed them not to leave Jerusalem, saying: 'You must wait for the gift which I told you about, promised by the Father. John baptized with water, but in a few days you shall be baptized with the Holy Spirit.'

When they were all together, they asked him: 'Lord, has the time now come when you will restore sovereignty to Israel?' Jesus replied: 'The dates and times of events are set by the Father, and it is not for you to know them. But the power of the Holy Spirit will come over you; and you will be my witnesses in Jerusalem, in all Judaea and Samaria, and to the ends of the earth.'

As the apostles were looking at Jesus, he was lifted up to heaven, and a cloud hid him from their sight. They stared into the sky as he went away. Then two men dressed in white suddenly appeared standing beside them, and said: 'Men of Galilee, why are looking up into the sky? This Jesus, who has been taken from you into heaven, will return in the same way that you saw him go.'

Acts 1.3–11

The coming of the Holy Spirit

On the day of Pentecost all the believers came together in one place. Suddenly a noise from the sky, like a violent wind, filled the whole house where they were sitting. Then they saw flames, like tongues of fire, which spread out and touched every person. They were all filled with the Holy Spirit, and began to speak in different languages, as the Spirit gave them power of expression.

Devout people, from every nation under heaven, were staying in Jerusalem; and when they heard the noise, a large crowd of them gathered. They were excited because each one heard his own language spoken. In amazement and wonder they exclaimed: 'Surely all these people speaking are Galileans! How is it that all of us hear them speaking in our own native languages? We are from Parthia, Media and Elam; from Mesopotamia, Judaea and Cappadocia; from Pontus and Asia, from Phrygia and Pamphylia, from Egypt and the regions of Libya near Cyrene. Some of us are visitors from Rome, both Jews and Gentiles converted to Judaism, and some are from Crete and Arabia. Yet all of us hear them speaking in our own languages about the great things which God has done.' They were all astonished and bewildered, and asked one another: 'What does this mean?'

Some, however, mocked the believers, saying: 'These people are drunk.'

Acts 2.1–13

Peter's address

Peter stood up with the other eleven apostles, and in a loud voice addressed the crowd: 'Fellow Jews and all who live in Jerusalem, hear me and take note of what I say. These people are not drunk, as you suppose; it is only nine o'clock in the morning! Let me speak to you about Jesus of Nazareth, a man whose divine authority was made known to you by all the miracles and wonders performed by God through him. You yourselves know this, for these things happened amongst you. In accordance with God's own will and plan, this man was put into your power, and you killed him, using heathen men to crucify him. But God raised him to life again, setting him free from the pangs of death, because it was impossible that death should hold him captive. And of this resurrection of Jesus we are all witnesses. Then, lifted up to the right hand of God, his Father, he received the Holy Spirit, as God had promised; and all that you now see and hear flows from the Spirit. May all the people of Israel know for certain that God has made this Jesus, whom you crucified, both Lord and Christ.'

When the people heard these words, they were cut to the heart, and asked Peter and the other apostles: 'What are we to do?' Peter replied: 'Repent, and be baptized, every one of you, in the name of Jesus the Christ; then your sins will be forgiven and you will receive the Holy Spirit. God made his promise to you and your children, to all who are in distant lands, and to everyone whom he is calling to himself.'

Acts 2.14–15, 22–24, 32–33, 36–39

Life among the believers

Peter spoke to the people at great length, using many arguments. 'Save yourselves from this crooked age,' he urged. Those who accepted his message, were baptized; and about three thousand people were added that day to the company of believers.

They met constantly to hear the apostles teach, and to enjoy the common life, breaking bread and praying. Many miracles and signs occurred through the apostles, and everyone was filled with awe. They agreed to hold all things in common, so they sold their property and possessions, and distributed the money among themselves according to each person's need. Day after day they gathered in the temple, and they ate together in their homes, sharing their food with glad and generous hearts, and praising God. They won the respect of everyone; and every day the Lord added new converts to their number.

Acts 2.40–47

The cripple at the temple

One day, when Peter and John were on their way to the temple at three in the afternoon, the hour for prayer, they passed a man who was being carried there. He had been a cripple from birth, and every day he was put by the temple entrance, known as the Beautiful Gate, to beg from people as they went in. When he saw Peter and John walking towards the temple, he begged from them. Peter and John fixed their eyes on him. 'Look at us,' Peter said. Expecting a gift from them, he looked intently. Peter continued: 'I have neither silver nor gold, but I shall give you what I have: in the name of Jesus Christ, get up and walk.' Peter grasped him by the right hand, helping him to stand up, and at once the man's feet and ankles became strong. He sprang to his feet and started to walk. Then he entered the temple with them, leaping and praising God as he went.

All the people present saw him walking and praising God. And when they recognized him as the man who used to sit begging at the Beautiful Gate, they were astonished and amazed at what had happened to him.

Acts 3.1—10

The seven helpers

Some time later, as the number of disciples continued to grow, those who spoke Greek made a complaint against those who spoke the Jewish language: they claimed that their widows were being overlooked in the daily distribution of funds. So the twelve apostles called the whole group of believers together, and said: 'It is not right for us to neglect the preaching of God's word in order to organize the daily distribution. So, brothers and sisters, choose seven men among you who are known to be full of the Holy Spirit and of wisdom, and we shall put them in charge of this matter. Then we can devote ourselves to prayer and to the work of preaching.'

The whole group accepted the proposal; and they elected Stephen, a man full of faith and the Holy Spirit, along with Philip, Prochurus, Nicanor, Timon, Parmenas and Nicolaus of Antioch, who had earlier been converted to Judaism. The group presented them to the apostles, who prayed and laid hands on them.

The word of God continued to spread, and the number of disciples in Jerusalem increased rapidly; many priests embraced the faith.

Acts 6. 1–7

The arrest of Stephen

Stephen, a man richly blessed by God and full of power, began to perform great miracles and signs among the people. A group from the Synagogue of Freedmen, which included former Jewish slaves from Cyrene and Alexandria, came forward and began to argue with Stephen; and they were joined by people from Cilicia and Asia. But the Spirit gave Stephen such wisdom that, when he spoke, they could not refute him. So they paid some men to say: 'We heard him speaking against Moses and against God!' In this way they stirred up the people, as well as the elders and teachers of the law. Then they seized Stephen and took him before the Council.

They brought in men to lie about Stephen; and they said to the Council: 'This man is constantly making speeches against the sacred temple and the law of Moses. We heard him say that Jesus of Nazareth will tear down the temple, and alter all the customs which came down to us from Moses.' The members of the Council looked intently at Stephen, and his face seemed to them like that of an angel.

The high priest asked Stephen: 'Is this true?' Stephen replied: 'How stubborn you are, with heathen hearts and deaf ears! Like your ancestors you have always resisted the Holy Spirit. Was there any prophet that your ancestors did not persecute? They killed those who long ago foretold the coming of God's righteous servant, and now you have betrayed and murdered him. You were given the law by God's angels, yet you have not obeyed it!'

Acts 6.8—7.1, 51–53

The stoning of Stephen

As the members of the Council listened to Stephen, they
began to grind their teeth with fury. But Stephen, filled with
the Holy Spirit, looked up to heaven and saw the glory of
God, with Jesus standing at God's right hand. 'Look,' he exclaimed, 'I can see heaven thrown open, and the Son of Man
standing at the right hand of God!'

At these words the members of the Council gave a great
shout, and covered their ears with their hands. Then together
they rushed towards him, threw him out of the city, and
hurled stones at him. They left their cloaks in the care of a
young man named Saul. As they were stoning Stephen, he
called out: 'Lord Jesus, receive my spirit!' He fell on his knees
and exclaimed: 'Lord, do not hold this sin against them.' And
with these words he died. Saul approved of his killing.

That day the church in Jerusalem began to suffer violent
persecution. All the believers, except the apostles, were scattered throughout the provinces of Judaea and Samaria. A
group of devout men, however, buried Stephen and cried in
mourning for him.

Saul himself sought to destroy the church. He went from
house to house, dragging out believers, both men and
women, and throwing them in prison.

Acts 7.54—8.3

The conversion of Saul

Saul went to the high priest and asked for letters addressed to the synagogues in Damascus; these authorized him to arrest any followers of the new way whom he found, both men and women, and bring them to Jerusalem.

While Saul was on the road to Damascus, approaching the city, suddenly a light from the sky flashed all around him. He fell to the ground and heard a voice saying: 'Saul, Saul, why are you persecuting me?' 'Tell me, Lord, who are you?' he asked. The voice said: 'I am Jesus, whom you are persecuting. Get up and go into the city, and you will be told what you must do.'

The men travelling with Saul stood speechless; they heard the voice, but could see no one. Saul rose from the ground, but when he opened his eyes he could see nothing; so they had to lead him to Damascus by the hand. He was blind for three days, and did not eat or drink.

Acts 9. 1–9

The baptism of Saul

In Damascus lived a believer called Ananias. He had a vision in which he heard the Lord say: 'Ananias!' He replied: 'Here I am, Lord,' The Lord said: 'Get up and go to the house of Judas in Straight Street, and ask there for a man from Tarsus named Saul. You will find him praying; and in a vision he has seen a man named Ananias coming in and laying hands on him to restore his sight.' 'Lord,' Ananias answered, 'I have often heard about this man and all the harm he has done to your people in Jerusalem. Now he is here with authority from the chief priests to arrest all who worship you.' The Lord said: 'Go. I have chosen this man to serve me, by making my name known to the nations and their kings, and to the people of Israel. I myself shall show him all he must suffer for my sake.'

So Ananias went to the house where Saul was, and laid hands on him. 'Brother Saul,' he said, 'the Lord Jesus, who appeared to you on the road as you were coming here, has sent me to you, so that you may recover your sight and be filled with the Holy Spirit.' At once scales seemed to fall from Saul's eyes, and he regained his sight. He got up and was baptized; and after taking some food his strength returned.

Saul – also known as Paul – stayed for some time with the disciples in Damascus. After only a few days he began preaching in the synagogues, proclaiming Jesus to be the Son of God. All who heard him were astounded, asking one another: 'Is not this the man who was in Jerusalem, hunting down the worshippers of Jesus?'

Acts 9.10–21a

The meeting in Jerusalem

Paul went to visit the apostles and elders in Jerusalem, urging them to accept Gentile converts into the church. But some of the believers who belonged to the party of the Pharisees objected, saying: 'The Gentiles must be circumcised and ordered to keep the law of Moses.'

The apostles and elders met to consider this question. After a long debate Peter stood up to address them: 'My friends, you know that long ago God chose me from among you to preach the gospel to the Gentiles, so they could hear and believe. And God, who can read every human heart, showed his approval by giving the Holy Spirit to the Gentiles, just as he had to us. He made no distinction between them and us; he purified their hearts by faith. So why do you put God to the test now, by laying on the shoulders of these converts a yoke which neither our ancestors nor we ourselves were able to bear? We believe that we are saved in the same way as they are: through the grace of the Lord Jesus.'

Then James rose and spoke: 'My friends, listen to me. In my judgement we should impose no irksome rules on the Gentiles who turn to God. Instead we should send them a letter, instructing them to abstain from food that is polluted by contact with idols, and from sexual immorality.'

Acts 15.4–11, 19–20a

In Thessalonica

Paul, with his companion Silas, travelled from place to place, preaching the gosepl. They arrived in Thessalonica. There was a synagogue in the city, and Paul went to the meetings there, holding discussions with the people. He quoted and expounded texts of Scripture, showing from them that the Christ must suffer and rise from the dead. He concluded: 'This Jesus, whom I am proclaiming to you, is the Christ.' Some were convinced and joined Paul and Silas, as did a large number of devout Gentiles and leading women.

The Jews became jealous. So they recruited some ruffians from the streets to form a mob, and these men soon set the whole city in an uproar. They began looking for Paul and Silas, in order to bring them before the people, and in their search they attacked the home of a Christian called Jason. But failing to find Paul and Silas, they dragged Jason himself and some other believers before the city authorities, shouting: 'These men have caused trouble everywhere, and now they have come to our city. Jason has been harbouring them; and all of them have been flouting the laws of the emperor by asserting that there is a rival king called Jesus.' The people became alarmed by these accusations, as did those in authority, who made Jason and the others pay a sum of money as security before releasing them.

Acts 17. 1–9

To Berea and Athens

As soon as darkness fell, the believers sent Paul and Silas to Berea; and when they arrived, they went to the synagogue. The people there were more open-minded than those in Thessalonica. Many believed, as did some Gentile women of high social standing and a number of Gentile men.

When the Jews of Thessalonica heard that the message of God had now been proclaimed by Paul in Berea, they followed him there to cause trouble by stirring up the crowd. The believers immediately sent Paul down to the coast, while Silas and Timothy stayed behind. When Paul arrived in Athens, he sent a message to Timothy and Silas, asking them to join him as soon as they could.

While Paul was waiting for them in Athens, he observed that the city was full of idols. He was outraged; so he held discussions, both in the synagogue with the Jewish and the Gentile worshippers, and in the public square where every day he accosted passers-by. Epicurean and Stoic philosophers also debated with him. Some said: 'What is this charlatan trying to say?' Others, having heard Paul preach about Jesus and the resurrection, answered: 'He seems to be talking about foreign gods.'

So they took Paul to the city council, the Areopagus, where they said to him: 'May we know this new doctrine that you are teaching? The ideas you expound are strange to us, and we should like to know what they mean.' The greatest amusement for the citizens of Athens was to hear and discuss the latest ideas.

Acts 17.10–11a, 12–21

Paul's speech to the Athenians

Paul stood up in front of the city council, and spoke: 'Men of Athens, I see that in religious matters you are extremely scrupulous. As I walked through your city looking at the objects of your worship, I noticed an altar bearing the inscription, "To an Unknown God". In fact the unknown God whom you revere, is the God whom I now proclaim to you.

'The God, who created the world and everything in it, and who is the Lord of heaven and earth, does not live in shrines made by human hands. Nor does he need anything that we can supply by our efforts, since he himself is the source of all things to all people, including life and breath. From a single stock he created the whole human race, to inhabit the entire earth; and for each nation he determined the eras of their history and the limits of their territory. His purpose was that they might seek him; and by searching for him they would find him. Indeed, he is close to us all.

'We are God's children. Thus we should not think that his nature is like an image in gold, silver or stone, shaped by human art and skill. God has overlooked the times of ignorance, and is now commanding men and women everywhere to repent.'

At the mention of rising from death some of them laughed. But others said: 'We want to hear you speak about this again.' So Paul left the meeting. Some people joined him, and became believers, including Dionysius, a member of the Council, and a woman called Damaris.

Acts 17.22–27, 29–30, 32–34

In Corinth

Paul now left Athens and went on to Corinth. There he met a Jew called Aquila, born in Pontus, and his wife Priscilla. They had recently arrived from Italy because the Emperor Claudius had ordered all Jews to leave Rome. They earned their living by making tents, as Paul did, and he made his home with them. Every sabbath he held discussions in the synagogue, trying to convert both Jews and Gentiles. Meanwhile Silas and Timothy arrived from Macedonia.

Paul devoted himself entirely to preaching, testifying to the Jews that Jesus is the Christ. When they turned against him and hurled insults at him, he took off his cloak and shook it in front of them, declaring: 'Let your blood be on you own heads; from now on I shall go to the Gentiles with a clear conscience.' With that he left them, and went to live with a Gentile called Titius Justus, who worshipped God devoutly; his house was next to the synagogue. Crispus, the president of the synagogue, became a believer in the Lord, together with his whole family; and many others in Corinth who heard the message also became believers, and were baptized.

One night the Lord appeared to Paul in a vision, and said: 'Do not be afraid; go on preaching and do not be silenced. I am with you, and no one can harm you, for many in this city are my people.' So Paul stayed there for a year and a half, teaching the word of God to the people.

Acts 18.1—11

In Ephesus

Finally, after such a long period in Corinth, Paul took leave of the believers there, and sailed for Syria, accompanied by Priscilla and Aquila. He had his head shaved at Cenchreae because of a vow he had made. When they reached Ephesus, he left Priscilla and Aquila, and went to the synagogue, where he talked with the Jews.

While he was in Ephesus, he met a group of people who had already turned to the Lord, and asked them: 'Did you receive the Holy Spirit when you became believers?' They replied: 'No, we have not even heard about the Holy Spirit.' 'Then how were you baptized?' Paul asked. 'With the baptism of John,' they answered. Paul said: 'The baptism of John was a sign of repentance, and he told the people who received it to put their trust in the one who was coming after him; and that person is Jesus.' On hearing this they were baptized in the name of the Lord Jesus. When Paul laid his hands on them, the Holy Spirit came down on them; and they began to speak in tongues of ecstasy, proclaiming God's word. This group numbered about twelve.

During the next three months Paul attended the synagogue, speaking forthrightly to the people about the kingdom of God. Some proved stubborn, refusing to believe, and they began to speak falsely about the way of the Lord to the congregation. So Paul left the synagogue, taking the believers with him, and held discussions each day in the lecture hall of Tyrannus. This continued for two years.

Acts 18.18–19; 19.2–10a

Riot in Ephesus

While Paul was in Ephesus, the Christian movement gave rise to a serious disturbance. A silversmith called Demetrius, who provided work for a large number of craftsmen making silver shrines of the goddess Artemis, called together his own craftsmen and others in the same trade. He said to them: 'As you know, our prosperity depends on this industry. Now you can see and hear for yourselves what this man Paul is doing. He claims that gods made by human hands are not gods at all, and he has perverted large numbers with his ideas, not only in Ephesus but in almost the whole province of Asia. Our line of business is in danger of getting a bad name, and also the temple of the great goddess Artemis may cease to command respect. Then soon the goddess herself, who is venerated in Asia and throughout the civilized world, would lose her prestige.'

As the craftsmen heard these words, they grew angry and started shouting: 'Great is Artemis of Ephesus!' The uproar spread through the whole city.

Eventually the town clerk calmed the crowd, saying: 'Citizens of Ephesus, all the world knows that our city of Ephesus is the guardian of the temple of the great Artemis, and of that image of her which fell from heaven. Since this is beyond dispute, you must do nothing reckless. These men have not robbed our temples or insulted our goddess. We could be accused of causing a riot by our behaviour today; and we have no excuse or reason for this.'

Acts 19.23–29a, 35–37, 40

The sleepy young man

When the disturbance was over, Paul called together the disciples, and gave them words of encouragement. Then he took leave of them and went on to Macedonia. He returned by way of Troas.

On Saturday evening Paul and the local believers gathered to break bread; and Paul, who was due to leave next day, addressed them. He carried on speaking until midnight, while numerous lamps burnt in the upstairs room where we were assembled. A young man called Eutychus, who was sitting on the window ledge, grew drowsy, and was finally overcome with sleep. He fell from the third storey to the ground; and when they picked him up, he was dead. Paul went down and threw himself on the boy. He clasped him in his arms, and declared: 'Do not distress yourselves; he is alive.' He then returned upstairs, broke bread and ate. Conversation continued until dawn, when Paul left. They took the boy home, greatly relieved that he was alive.

Paul arrived in Assos, and boarded ship. Paul decided to sail past Ephesus so as to lose no time in the province of Asia; he was eager to reach Jerusalem, if possible, by the day of Pentecost. The boat called at Miletus, where he sent a message to Ephesus, inviting the elders of the church to come and meet him.

Acts 20.1, 5, 7–12, 14, 16–17

Paul's address to the Ephesian elders

When the elders of the church in Ephesus arrived at Miletus, Paul addressed them: 'You know how I spent my entire time with you, from the day that I first set foot in the province of Asia. You know that I did not hold back in serving you, that I delivered God's word to you, and that I taught you both in public and in your own homes. To Jews and Gentiles alike I urged repentance before God and faith in our Lord Jesus. Now, as you see, the Spirit is prompting me to go to Jerusalem. I do not know what will happen to me there; I only know that in city after city the Holy Spirit has warned me that imprisonment and hardship await me. But I count my own life as worth nothing; my only desire is to finish the race, completing the work that the Lord Jesus has given me, which is to bear witness to the gospel of divine grace.

'You are shepherds of the Lord's church, which he won for himself by his blood; so keep watch over yourselves and over all the flock which the Holy Spirit has put in your care. I know that when I have gone, fierce wolves will come among you, and will show no mercy to your flock. Even from your own number some will distort the truth in order to gain disciples for themselves. So be on your guard, remembering how with tears I never ceased to guide you night and day for three years.'

Acts 20.18–24, 28–31

Paul's example and commendation

Paul continued: 'I commend you to God and the message of his grace, which can build you up and give you the blessings that God has for all his people. I have never asked anyone for money or clothes, but, as you know, I have worked with these hands of mine to earn what I and my companions have needed. I have always shown you that by working hard in this way we can fulfil our duty of supporting the weak. Let us remember the words that the Lord Jesus himself said: "There is more happiness in giving than in receiving."'

When he had finished speaking, he knelt down with them and prayed. Then they hugged and kissed him, with tears in their eyes, and the sadness of his parting was even greater because he had said they would never see him again.

They escorted Paul to the ship. When he and his companions arrived in Jerusalem, the believers welcomed them warmly. The next day Paul went with his companions to visit James; all the elders were present. Paul greeted them and reported in detail all that God had done among the Gentiles through his work.

Acts 20.32–38; 21.17–19

Paul's arrest

Paul was in the temple in Jerusalem, at the end of the period of purification, when some Jews from the province of Asia saw him. They stirred up the crowd and seized Paul, shouting: 'Men of Israel, help us. This is the man who attacks our people, our law and this temple. He is spreading his message everywhere. And now he has even brought Gentiles into the temple and defiled this holy place!' They had previously seen Trophimus from Ephesus with him in the city, and assumed that Paul had brought him into the temple.

Soon the whole city was in turmoil, with people running towards the temple from all directions. They grabbed Paul and dragged him out of the temple, shutting the temple doors behind them. They intended to kill him; but a report of the riot in Jerusalem was sent to the commander of the Roman troops, and he immediately rushed with some officers and soldiers towards the crowd. When the people saw the commander and his troops, they stopped beating Paul. The commander went to Paul and arrested him, ordering him to be bound with two chains. Then he asked: 'Who is this man, and what has he done?' Some in the crowd shouted one thing and some another; and as the commander in the confusion could not find out the truth, he ordered his troops to take Paul to the fort. When they reached the steps of the fort, the soldiers had to carry Paul because the crowd was so violent, coming after him and screaming, 'Kill him'.

Acts 21.27–36

Paul's trial before the Council

The commander wanted to know accurately what charges the Jews were bringing against Paul. So the next day he summoned the chief priests and the whole Council; then he ordered that Paul be unshackled and brought down to stand before them.

Paul looked straight at the members of the Council, and said: 'My brothers, to this day I have always conducted myself before God with a perfectly clear conscience.' At this the high priest Ananias ordered Paul to be struck on the mouth.

Paul knew that some members of the Council were Sadducees and others were Pharisees. 'My brothers,' Paul said to the Council, 'I am a Pharisee, and was born and bred a Pharisee; and the issue at this trial is our hope that the dead will rise to life.' At this the Pharisees and Sadducees started to quarrel, and the Council was split between these two parties. The Sadducees say that there is no resurrection, no angel or spirit, while the Pharisees believe in all three. Members of the Council began shouting at one another, and finally some teachers of the law belonging to the party of the Pharisees stood up, and declared: 'We find no fault with this man; perhaps an angel or spirit really has spoken to him.' As the dispute became even fiercer, the commander was afraid that Paul would be torn to pieces. So he ordered his troops to go into the crowd, pull Paul out, and take him back to the fort.

That night the Lord appeared to Paul, and said: 'Keep up your courage. You have borne witness for me in Jerusalem, and now you must do the same in Rome.'

Acts 22.30—23.2, 6–11

Paul's trials before the governors

The commander called two of his centurions, and said: 'By nine o'clock tonight be ready to leave for Caesarea, with two hundred troops, seventy horsemen and two hundred guards. Provide horses for Paul, and deliver him unharmed to Felix the governor.' The soldiers carried out their orders.

After some days in Caesarea, Paul was summoned to appear before Felix and his wife Drusilla, who was Jewish. Felix allowed Paul to talk about faith in Christ Jesus. But when Paul began to speak about morality, self-control and the coming day of judgement, Felix became alarmed, exclaiming: 'Enough for now; I shall send for you again when I find it convenient.' He hoped that Paul would bribe him, so he sent for him frequently. After two years Felix was succeeded as governor by Porcius Festus. Felix left Paul in prison in order to gain favour with the Jews.

Three days after his arrival in the province, Festus went from Caesarea to Jerusalem, where the chief priests and Jewish leaders laid before him their charges against Paul. They urged Festus to support their case and have Paul transferred to Jerusalem; they had plans to kill him on the way. Festus returned to Caesarea, and summoned Paul, who said: 'I have committed no offence against the Jewish law, against the temple, or against the Roman emperor. I appeal to the emperor.'

Festus, after conferring with his advisers, replied: 'You have appealed to the emperor; to the emperor you will go.'

Acts 23.23–24; 24.24—25.3, 6a, 8, 11b–12

In Rome

When he arrived in Rome, Paul was allowed to live privately with a soldier guarding him. Three days later Paul called together the local Jewish leaders. When they had gathered, he said to them: 'My brothers, although I did nothing against our people or against the customs which we received from our ancestors, I was arrested in Jerusalem and then handed over to the Romans. After questioning me they wanted to release me, because they found I had committed no capital offence. But the Jews objected, and I was forced to appeal to the emperor. I myself have no accusation to make against my own people. I am now in chains for the sake of him on whom the people of Israel place their hope. Thus I have asked to see and talk to you.'

They replied: 'We want to hear your ideas directly from you. All we know about your sect is that no one has a good word to say for it.'

So they fixed a date, and on that day a large number of them came to the house where Paul was staying. From dawn until dusk Paul expounded his message about the kingdom of God, and tried to convince them about Jesus by appealing to the law of Moses and to the prophets. Some were won over by his argument, while others remained sceptical.

Paul stayed there for two years at his own expense, welcoming all who visited him. He proclaimed the kingdom of God and taught the truth about the Lord Jesus Christ, speaking openly and without hindrance.

Acts 28.16–20, 22–24, 30–31

Paul was a tireless traveller and preacher, founding Christian communities throughout the Mediterranean world. To keep in touch with them, and to guide them through difficulties, he wrote letters to be read aloud to them. Along with the four Gopsels, Paul's letters form the bulk of the New Testament, which since the second century CE has been the sacred text of Christianity. Paul's interpretation of the death and resurrection of Christ became the heart of Christian teaching.

The letters of other early Christian leaders, most notably James, Peter and John, are also included in the New Testament. It is commonly assumed that John is the same as the writer of the fourth Gospel.

The practice of writing letters to churches continued beyond the period of the New Testament. Clement (d. c. 100), the leader of the Roman church at the end of the first century, wrote a famous letter to the church in Corinth, founded by Paul; as in Paul's time they were beset by disputes, and, like Paul, Clement urges unity. Before his conversion Clement was probably a slave; he then converted his owners, who freed him.

Ignatius (d. c. 110) was leader of the church in Antioch, and was condemned for his faith; he was then taken in chains to Rome, to be eaten by lions in the public arena. During his journey he wrote letters to various churches as he passed nearby; in them he describes his feelings about his impending death.

Christ's reconciling death

Now that we have been put right with God by faith, we are at peace with God through our Lord Jesus Christ, who has given us access to that divine grace in which we now live; and we boast of our hope of sharing God's glory. Let us also boast of our present sufferings, because we know that suffering produces endurance, endurance brings God's approval, and his approval causes hope. This hope will not be disappointed, because, through his gift of the Holy Spirit, God has flooded our hearts with his love.

When we were still helpless, Christ died for the wicked, at the time God chose. Few would be willing to die even for a righteous person, though for a truly good man one might lay down one's life. But the proof of God's love for us is that Christ died for us while we were still sinners. By his sacrificial death we have now been put right with God; thus we shall all the more certainly be saved through him from God's final retribution. If, when we were God's enemies, we were reconciled to him through the death of his Son, we can be all the more certain that being now reconciled, we shall be saved by Christ's life! But that is not all: we also rejoice in God through our Lord Jesus, who has reconciled us to God.

Paul: Romans 5. 1–11

Dying and rising with Christ

What are we to say, then? Shall we remain in sin, so that God's grace will increase? Certainly not! We have died to sin, so how can we go on living in it? Surely you know that when we were baptized into union with Christ Jesus, we were baptized into his death. By our baptism, then, we were buried with him, sharing his death, in order that, as Christ was raised from death by the glorious power of the Father, so also we might begin a new life.

Since we have become one with him in dying as he did, so we shall be one with him in being raised to life as he was. We know that our old self has been crucified with Christ, in order that the power of sin might be destroyed; thus we are set free from slavery to sin. Death, of course, breaks the chains of sin. In dying with Christ, we believe we shall also live with him, because we know that Christ has been raised from death and will never die again. Death can no longer rule over him. By his death he died to sin once and for all; and, by his risen life, he lives for God. In the same way you must regard yourselves as dead to sin and alive to God, in union with Christ Jesus.

Paul: Romans 6.1–11

Children of God

Those who do not possess the Spirit of Christ, do not belong to Christ. But if Christ lives within you, you have been put right with God: even though your body is dead because of sin, your spirit is alive. Moreover, if the Spirit of God, who raised Jesus from death, lives within you, then God will also give new life to your mortal bodies through his Spirit.

So then, my friends, our old nature has no claim on us; we have no obligation to live according to its wishes. If you do submit to its wishes, you will die. But if by the Spirit you put to death the base desires of the body, you will live.

All who are led by the Spirit of God, are sons and daughters of God. The Spirit that you have received is not a spirit of slavery, causing you to be afraid. Instead the Spirit makes you God's children, enabling you to cry out to God: 'Father, Father!' The Spirit of God joins with our spirits to declare that we are children of God. And if we are children, then we are heirs: we are heirs of God, and so fellow-heirs with Christ, sharing his suffering in order to share his glory.

Paul: Romans 8.9b—17

Groans of prayer

I believe that our suffering now cannot be compared with the glory that is in store for us. All creation is eagerly waiting for God's children to be revealed. Creation has been frustrated, not by its own choice, but by the will of God; and God's intention was that creation itself would be set free from its slavery to decay, and share in the glorious freedom of his children. We know that until the present time the whole of creation has been groaning, as if suffering the pain of childbirth. And we, who have received the Spirit as the first of God's gifts, also groan inwardly, as we wait eagerly for God to make us his children, setting us free from death. With this hope we were saved. If we were to see what we hope for, that would not be real hope – since we cannot hope for something we already see. But if we hope for something we do not yet see, then in waiting for it we show our endurance.

In all this the Spirit strengthens us, weak as we are. We do not even know how we should pray, but the Spirit himself pleads to God for us through our wordless groans. And God, who sees into our hearts, knows what the Spirit means, because the Spirit pleads for God's people in accordance with God's will. We know that in all things God works for good with those who love him.

Paul: Romans 8.18–28a

God's love for his people

With all this in mind, what can we say? If God is on our side, who can be against us? God did not spare his own Son, but offered him for us all. So will he not freely lavish every other gift upon us? Who can bring any charge against those whom God has chosen? God himself declares them innocent. Who will pass judgement? Not Christ, who died, and, furthermore, was raised to life, and is now at the right hand of God, pleading for us. What, then, can separate us from the love of Christ? Can hardship or distress? Can persecution? Can lack of food and clothing? Can the threat of violence, or violence itself? Whatever happens, we have complete victory through him who loved us.

I am convinced that nothing can separate us from the love of God. Nothing in life or death, no angels or spiritual powers, nothing in the present world or still to come, neither the world above nor the world below, nothing in all creation can come between us and God's love, which is ours through Christ Jesus our Lord.

Paul: Romans 8.31—39

Living sacrifice

I implore you, my brothers and sisters, by the mercy of God to offer yourselves to him as a living sacrifice, dedicated to his service and pleasing to him; in offering yourselves you are truly worshipping him. Do not conform to the standards of the world, but let God transform you inwardly by renewing your minds. Then you will be able to discern the will of God, and thus know what is good, pleasing to him and holy.

Through the grace which God has granted me, I urge each one of you not to think too highly of yourself, but be modest, judging yourself according to the measure of faith which God has given you. In a single human body there are many limbs and organs, all with different functions. In the same way we are one body in union with Christ, joined to one another as limbs and organs. So let us use the various gifts bestowed on us by God's grace. If our gift is prophecy, for example, we should prophesy as our faith prompts us; if it is practical service, we should devote ourselves to serving others; if it is teaching, we should teach; if it is the gift of counsel, we should counsel. When you give to others, do it with a generous heart; when you lead others, do it with enthusiasm; when you help others in distress, do it cheerfully.

Paul: Romans 12.1—8

Sincere love

Let love be sincere. Hate what is evil, and hold fast to what is good. Express your love for one another in mutual affection. Regard others as more important than yourself. Work hard and do not be lazy. Serve the Lord with your whole heart. Let your hope keep you joyful. Stand firm in your troubles. Pray at all times. Open your homes to strangers. Share what you have with any of God's people in need.

Bless those who persecute you; never curse them, but ask God's blessings on them. Rejoice with those who rejoice, and weep with those who weep. Care for everyone equally. Do not be proud, but undertake the most humble tasks. Do not think of yourself as wise.

Never pay back evil for evil. Direct your efforts towards what all consider to be good. As far as you are able, be at peace with everyone. My dear friends, never take revenge.

Paul: Romans 12.9–19a

Love and the law's fulfilment

The only debt you owe to one another is love; discharge this debt fully. Those who love their neighbours, fulfil every demand of the law. The commandments not to commit adultery, not to murder and steal, not to desire what belongs to others, and the rest, are summed up in the single command: 'Love your neighbour as yourself'. If you love someone, you cannot do them wrong; so to love is to obey the whole law.

Remember that the time has now come for you to wake from sleep. The moment of our salvation is nearer to us now than when we first believed. The night is almost over; dawn is near. So let us throw off everything that belongs to the night, and equip ourselves for the light. Let us live in the light of day, behaving decently; let there be no drunken orgies, no promiscuity or vice, no quarrels or jealousies. Wear Jesus Christ as your armour, giving your sinful nature no opportunity to satisfy its desires.

Paul: Romans 13.8−14

Weakness in faith

Welcome those who are weak in faith, but do not argue with
them about points of doubt. For example, one person may
have sufficient faith to eat any kind of food, while another,
who is weak in faith, eats only vegetables. Those who eat
freely should not despise those who do not; nor should those
who do not eat freely pass judgement on those who do. God
accepts them all. Who are you to judge someone else's servants? Their own Master decides whether they succeed or fail;
and they will succeed, because he will uphold them.

Similarly, some think that certain days are holier than
others, while some regard all days as equal. People should
make up their own minds. Those who honour a certain day,
honour the Lord. In the same way those who eat freely can
honour the Lord by giving thanks to God for their food. And
those who refuse to eat certain things can also honour the
Lord by giving thanks to God.

Let us, therefore, stop judging one another. Instead, let
us decide never to do anything that would make a fellow
disciple stumble or fall into sin.

Paul: Romans 14. 1–6, 13

Mutual acceptance

Let us always seek ways that lead to peace, and ways in which
we strengthen one another. Those of us who are strong in
faith should bear as our own burden the tender scruples of
the weak. We should not try to please ourselves, but rather
please our brothers and sisters, doing whatever will suit
them, and in this way build up our common life. May God,
the source of patience and encouragement, give you all the
same purpose, which is to follow the example of Christ Jesus.
Then with one mind and voice you will praise the God and
Father of our Lord Jesus Christ. Accept one another for the
glory of God, as Christ has accepted you.

                              Paul: Romans 14.19; 15.1–2, 5–7

Divine folly and weakness

The message of the cross is folly to those who are being lost; but to us on the way to salvation it is the power of God. Where does that leave the philosophers, the scholars, the skilful debaters of this world? God has shown up this world's wisdom as folly.

God in his wisdom has made it impossible for people to know him by means of their own wisdom. Instead God chose to save believers through the folly of the gospel. Jews demand miracles and Greeks look for wisdom, but we proclaim Christ nailed to the cross. To the Jews this is an offence, to the Gentiles it is folly; yet to those who are called, Jews and Greeks alike, Christ is both the power of God and the wisdom of God. The folly of God is wiser than human wisdom, and the weakness of God stronger than human strength.

My brothers and sisters, consider what sort of people you are, whom God has called. Few of you are wise by human standards, few of you are powerful or of noble birth. Yet God chose those whom this world counts as fools to shame the wise; and he chose those whom this world counts as weak to shame the powerful. He has chosen those whom the world despises, treats with contempt and counts as worthless, in order to overthrow the existing order. Human pride has no place in the presence of God. God has brought you into union with Christ Jesus, and he has made Christ our wisdom. In Christ we have salvation, holiness and freedom.

Paul: 1 Corinthians 1.18, 20–30

Love

I may speak in human or angelic tongues, but if I have no love, my speech is no more than a booming gong or a clanging cymbal. I may have the gift of prophecy and the knowledge of every hidden truth; I may have faith great enough to move mountains; but if I have no love, I am nothing. I may give all I possess to those in need, I may give my body to be burnt, but if I have no love, I gain nothing.

Love is patient and kind; love is never jealous; love is never boastful, conceited or rude; love is never selfish or quick to take offence; love keeps no record of wrongs; love takes no pleasure in the sins of others, but delights in the truth. Love is always ready to make allowances, to trust, to hope and to endure, whatever may happen.

Love is eternal. Prophecies will cease; tongues of ecstasy will fall silent; knowledge will vanish. Our knowledge and our prophecy alike are partial; and when wholeness comes, that which is partial disappears.

When I was a child, I spoke like a child, had childish emotions, thought like a child. When I grew up, I finished with all childish ways. At present we see only dim reflections in a mirror; but one day we shall see face to face. My knowledge now is partial; then it will be whole, like God's knowledge of me.

These three last forever: faith, hope and love. And the greatest of these is love.

Paul: 1 Corinthians 13.1–13

The resurrection body

You may ask how the dead are raised, and in what kind of body. How foolish! The seed you sow in the ground does not come to life unless it first dies. And what you sow is not the full-grown plant, that will later grow up, but a bare seed of wheat or some other grain. God provides that seed with the body he wishes; to each seed he gives its own particular body. That is how it will be when the dead are raised to life. The body that is buried in the ground is mortal; but when raised it will be immortal. When it is buried, the body is ugly and weak; when raised, it will be beautiful and strong. When buried, the body is physical; when raised, it will be spiritual.

Let me unfold a mystery. We shall not all die, but when the last trumpet sounds we shall be changed in an instant, as quickly as the blinking of an eye. When the trumpet sounds, the dead will be raised immortal, and we shall be changed; this mortal body will become immortal.

Therefore, my dear brothers and sisters, stand firm and steady; and devote all your strength to the Lord's work. You can be sure that in the Lord your labours can never be wasted.

Paul: 1 Corinthians 15.35–38, 42–44, 51–53a, 58

Christ's reconciling death

We recognize that Jesus Christ died for us all, and therefore all people share in his death. For this reason the love of Christ rules us. He died for all, so that those who live should no longer live for themselves, but for him who died and was raised to life for their sake.

Thus we do not judge anyone by worldly standards. Even if at one time we judged Christ by worldly standards, we no longer do so. Anyone who is united with Christ is a new creation; the old order has gone, the new order has begun. All this has been done by God. He has reconciled us to himself through Christ, and has entrusted us with the task of reconciling the whole human race to himself, no longer keeping an account of people's sins. We are Christ's ambassadors; God himself is making his appeal through us. We implore all people in Christ's name to be reconciled to God. Christ was innocent of sin, yet for our sake God made him a victim of sin, that in union with him we can share his righteousness.

Paul: 2 Corinthians 5.14–21

The cheerful giver

Remember that the one who sows few seeds will have a small crop; and the one who sows many seeds will have a large crop. You should each give as you have freely decided, not reluctantly or out of compulsion; God loves a cheerful giver. God is able to provide for you in abundance, so that you will always have enough for your own needs, and also enough for every good cause.

God, who supplies seed to sow and bread to eat, will give ample seed for you to sow; and he will make it grow, so that your generosity will produce a rich spiritual harvest. You will always be rich enough to be generous, so that many will thank God for your gifts. This service will not only meet the material needs of God's people, but also will produce a flood of gratitude to God. Your help to others will be proof to them of your faith; so when people see how humbly you obey God and how loyally you proclaim Christ's gospel, they will offer praise to God. And they will pray for you, expressing to God their affection for you.

Paul: 2 Corinthians 9.6–8, 10–14a

Fruits of the Spirit

Christ has set us free, so let us remain free. Stand firm, refusing to submit again to the yoke of slavery. My brothers and sisters, you have been called to freedom, but do not use your freedom as a licence to indulge your desires. Instead serve one another in love.

I tell you, let the Spirit direct your lives, and then you will no longer yield to self-indulgence. The behaviour that results from self-indulgence is plain: sexual vice, indecency and debauchery; the worship of idols and witchcraft; conflict and rivalry; jealousy, anger and selfish ambition; division into parties and factions; mutual envy; drunken orgies and the like. I warn you, as I have warned you before, that those who behave in this way will never inherit the kingdom of God.

But the fruits of the Spirit are love, joy, peace, patience, kindness, goodness, fidelity, humility and self-control. We who belong to Christ Jesus have crucified our old nature, putting to death its passions and desires. And the Spirit has given us new life. So let the Spirit direct our lives.

Paul: Galatians 5.1, 13, 16, 19–23a, 24–25

Family of love

I fall on my knees before the Father, from whom every family in heaven and on earth receives its name. I pray that from the abundance of his glory he may give you power through his Spirit to be inwardly strong, and that through faith Christ may live in your hearts. May you have deep roots and firm foundations in Christ's love, so, together with all God's people, you may have the power to grasp the breadth and length, the height and depth of that love. May you know Christ's love, even though it is beyond all knowledge. May you be filled with the fullness of God.

As a prisoner for the Lord's sake, I urge you to live up to the standards to which God has called you. Be always humble, gentle and patient, accepting one another's weaknesses in a spirit of love. Take every care to make fast with bonds of peace the unity that the Spirit gives. There is one body and one Spirit, just as there is one hope that is the goal to which God beckons you. There is one Lord, one faith, one baptism; one God and Father of all, who is over all, through all and in all.

Paul: Ephesians 3.14–19; 4.1–6

Health in spirit, soul and body

We beg you, brothers and sisters, to pay respect to those who labour so hard among you as your leaders and advisers in the Lord. Hold them in the highest esteem and affection for the work they do.

Live at peace among yourselves. We urge you, brothers and sisters, to rebuke the idle, encourage the timid, support the weak, and be patient with everyone. Ensure that no one tries to repay evil with evil. Always aim to do what is best for each other and for all people.

Be joyful at all times, pray continually, and give thanks in all circumstances; this is what God wants from you in Christ Jesus.

Do not stifle the words of inspiration, and do not treat the gift of prophecy with contempt. Test all that is said, holding on to what is good, and avoiding every kind of evil.

May the God of peace make you perfect and holy in every way. May he keep you healthy in spirit, soul and body, so that you are free from fault when our Lord Jesus Christ comes. He who has called you will do this, because he is faithful.

Pray also for us, brothers and sisters. Greet all your fellow believers with the kiss of peace.

Paul: 1 Thessalonians 5.12–26

Practical religion

Be quick to listen, but slow to speak and slow to become angry. Human anger does not promote divine justice. Rid yourselves of all sordid habits and all evil self-indulgence; and meekly accept the message planted in your hearts, which has power to save you.

Yet be sure to act on what you hear; do not merely listen, and so deceive yourselves. Whoever listens to the message, but does not put it into practice, is like a man looking in a mirror at his own features; and when he has seen his face, he goes off and promptly forgets it. But those who look closely at the perfect law, which sets people free, and do not turn away, will remember what they see; and when they act on it, they will find happiness.

Those who regard themselves as religious, but do not control their tongues, deceive themselves; their religion is futile. In the eyes of God the Father, pure and genuine religion consists in caring for orphans and widows in trouble, and in remaining uncorrupted by the world.

James 1.19–27

Human equality

My brothers and sisters, as believers in our Lord Jesus Christ, who reigns in glory, you must never treat people differently according to their outward appearance. For instance, two strangers come to your meeting, one wearing fine clothes and a gold ring, the other dressed in dirty rags. Suppose you show more respect to the well-dressed man, offering him one of the best seats, while you tell the poor man to sit on the floor by your feet. Then you are making judgements according to corrupt standards, and you will soon be creating similar distinctions among yourselves.

Listen, my brothers and sisters! God has chosen those who are poor in the eyes of the world to be rich in faith, and to possess the kingdom that he has promised to those who love him. And yet you dishonour the poor. You yourselves are oppressed by the rich, and dragged before judges by them. The rich insult the good name that has been given to you.

James 2.1–7

Patience and prayer

Be patient, my brothers and sisters, until the Lord comes. Look at the patience of the farmer, as he waits for the autumn and spring rains to make his crop grow. You too must be patient, keeping your hopes high, as you wait for the Lord; he will come soon.

Those among you who are in trouble should pray. Those who are joyful should sing praises. Those who are ill should send for the elders of the church to pray, and to anoint them with oil in the name of the Lord. Prayers offered in faith will heal those who are sick; the Lord will restore them to health, and the sins they have committed will be forgiven. Therefore confess your sins to one another, and pray for one another that you may be healed. The prayers of the righteous have a powerful effect.

My friends, if one of you strays from the truth and another one brings that person back, you may be sure of this: those who rescue sinners from their error save the sinners' souls from death, and cancel a multitude of sins.

James 5.7–8, 13–16, 19–20

A spiritual temple

Rid yourselves of all spite, deceit, hypocrisy, envy and malicious talk. Like new-born babies, you should thirst for pure spiritual milk, so that you will grow up to salvation.

Come to the Lord, the living stone rejected by human beings as worthless, but chosen by God as precious. Become living stones yourselves, to be built into a spiritual temple; and then form a holy priesthood to offer spiritual sacrifices acceptable to God through Jesus Christ. You are a chosen race, a royal priesthood, a holy nation. You are the people of God, who called you out of darkness into his marvellous light, in order to sing his praise. Once you belonged to no one; now you belong to God. Once you were ignorant of God's mercy; now you have received his mercy.

1 Peter 2.1–2, 4–5, 9–10

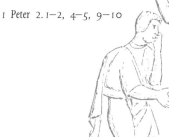

Good shepherds

As an elder myself, I appeal to the elders of your community. I am a witness of Christ's sufferings, and shall share the glory that is to be revealed. I urge you to care for the flock of which God has made you shepherd. Serve them not out of duty, but with a willing heart, as God wants; and work not for money, but out of genuine devotion. Do not give orders to those in your charge, but guide your flock by your own example. So when the chief Shepherd appears, you will receive a crown that never fades.

In the same way, the younger people should give respect to the older; and you should all serve one another wearing humility as an apron. Humble yourselves under God's mighty hand, so that in due time he will lift you up. Unload your anxieties on him, because he cares for you.

Be alert and sober; your enemy, the devil, roams about like a roaring lion, seeking someone to devour. Resist him, firm in your faith, and remember that your fellow Christians in all the world are enduring the same kind of suffering. After you have suffered a little while, the God of all grace, who calls you to his eternal glory in union with Christ, will himself restore and strengthen you, setting you on a firm foundation.

I write you this brief letter with the help of Silas, whom I regard as a faithful brother, in order to encourage you, and to bear witness to the true grace of God.

1 Peter 5.1–5a, 6–10, 12

Darkness and light

The darkness is passing away, and the true light is already shining. Those who say they are in the light, but hate their fellow believers, are still in darkness. But those who love their fellow believers live in the light; they will not cause others to stumble into sin. Those who hate their fellow believers are in darkness; they walk in the dark, not knowing where they are going, because the darkness has made them blind.

Do not love the world or the things that belong to the world. Those who love the world do not love the Father. The things of the world that pander to our physical appetites, enticing us to self-indulgence and appealing to selfish ambition, come not from the Father, but from the world itself. The world with all its pleasures is passing away; but those who obey God will live forever.

1 John 2.8b–11, 15–17

Perfect love

Dear friends, let us love one another, since love comes from God. Everyone who loves is a child of God, and knows God. But those who do not love are ignorant of God, because God is love. God showed his love for us by sending his only Son into the world, that we might have life through him. This is what love is: not that we have loved God, but that he loved us, and sent his Son to expiate our sins. If this is how God loves us, dear friends, we should love one another. No one has ever seen God, but if we love one another, he himself lives within us; his love is made perfect in us.

God is love; those who live in love live in God, and God lives in them. There is no fear in love; perfect love banishes all fear. Love has not been made perfect in anyone who is afraid, because fear implies punishment. We love because God first loved us. Christ has given us this command: those who love God must also love their fellow believers.

1 John 4.7–12, 16b, 18–19, 21

Mutual dependence

Think of soldiers in the field of battle; they must obey their commanders promptly and eagerly. Not everyone can be a commander, and yet someone must take this role. So it is in the Christian community; the leaders cannot exist without the followers, and the followers cannot exist without the leaders.

Indeed, this principle of mutual dependence applies to every aspect of our common life. If the strong are to grow in love, they must protect and care for the weak; and if the weak are to grow in humility, they must respect the strong. The rich should rejoice in being able to help the poor; and the poor should thank God for the generosity of the rich.

If you are wise, show your wisdom by good deeds, and not by words. If you are modest, let others praise you for your modesty, rather than proclaiming it yourself. If you are able to control your sexual desires, and thus remain single, do not brag about it; remember that self-control is a gift from God, to be used in his service.

Remember, my brothers and sisters, our origin. God brought from nothing into his universe; even before our birth he had planned how he would bless us. We owe everything to him; and so on every count we should give thanks to him.

Those who are ignorant and foolish may mock and ridicule us, in order to boost their own self-esteem. But what harm can they do to us? What harm can anyone on earth really do to us?

Clement of Rome: Corinthians 1.37–39

The path of love and the gate of life

When there is disunity amongst us, we should lose no time in putting matters right. We should fall on our knees before our Maker, weeping with shame, and implore him to pardon us; and we should beg him to lead us back onto the path of love. This is the path that leads to the gate of life. There are many gates standing open, through which we might pass, but the gate of life is the gate of Christ – and he will bless all who enter.

Go about your duties in such a manner that you never cause disunity. You may possess deep insight; you may be capable of expounding many divine mysteries; you may be wise and sound in judgement; you may be an example of virtue in all you do. But the higher your reputation stands, the humbler you should be. Moreover, your eyes should be fixed on the good of the whole community, and never on your own advantage.

If your heart is truly loving, then obey the commandments of Christ. Who can describe the power of love? Who can express its majesty and beauty? No tongue can relate the heights to which love can carry us. Love binds us to God. Love casts a veil over countless sins. There is no limit to the endurance of love, and no end to its patience. Love is free of both servility and arrogance. Love hates divisions and discord, and takes delight in friendship and harmony. Through love God's people are made perfect.

Clement of Rome: Corinthians 1.48–49

Open confession

Let us beg forgiveness for all our misdoings – for all the sins that the evil within us has prompted us to commit. Those who have caused friction and discord within the community should throw themselves on God, in the hope that he will have mercy on them. If people truly love and revere God, they would prefer to endure suffering themselves, than see others suffer; and they would prefer to take blame onto themselves, than see our proud tradition of harmony be sullied. It is far better for people to admit their faults, honestly and openly, than to harden their hearts.

Do any of you possess a noble mind? Are any among you compassionate? Do any of you overflow with love? Let such a person say to the church: 'It is I who caused disorder, friction and discord among you. I shall remove myself; I shall go wherever you send me; I shall do anything that you demand. My only desire is that there should be peace among you.' Anyone who does this, will be honoured by Christ – and will truly be a citizen of heaven.

For my part, I pray for those who have fallen into sin, asking that they may be given the humility to surrender themselves to the will of God. If they do so, God will be merciful – and so, I believe, will you, his church. My friends, do not resent the guidance of others; mutual correction is wholly beneficial.

Clement of Rome: Corinthians 1.51, 54, 56

Absolute unity

All things must come to an end. There are two alternatives before us: life and death. Each one of us will either live or die. Two different coinages are in circulation, God's coinage and the world's, each with its distinctive stamp. Some people choose the world's coinage; and they will die. Other people choose to carry God's coinage: they will die with Christ on the cross – and so live.

For God's sake I urge you to have a single heart and mind. Let your leader act not on his own behalf, but on God's; and let his helpers be honest and diligent – and so worthy of the trust that has been vested in them. Remember that all of you are servants of Jesus Christ, who was with the Father for all eternity, and has in these last days revealed himself to humanity. Strive to conform your will to God's will. Show kindness and consideration to one another. Never allow selfish emotions to affect your attitude to others; simply love one another constantly, after the example of Jesus Christ himself. Allow nothing to exist among you which could cause divisions amongst you; maintain absolute unity between the leader, the helpers and the people. Through unity corruption can be avoided.

Ignatius of Antioch: Magnesians 5, 6

Impending martyrdom

God has filled me with courage about my impending martyrdom. But I do not wish to boast, for fear that boasting would undermine me. I tell myself that I should feel apprehensive, and that I should deafen my ears to those who flatter me. Indeed, the words of flatterers are like whips on my back; for, although I yearn for martyrdom, I am unsure of whether I am worthy of it. So I desperately need to acquire humility.

I could write to you on glorious and heavenly topics. But, since you are infants in faith, I fear that such words would be harmful to you; they would stick in your throats, and you would be unable to digest them. As for myself, the chains binding my body enhance my capacity to understand the heavenly mysteries; I can see clearly that which is unseen by the human eye. Nonetheless I do not count myself as a true disciple of Christ. I remind myself constantly of how far I fall short – knowing that, if I regarded myself as already perfect, I should indeed fall short of God.

Ignatius of Antioch:
Trallians 4, 5

A human sacrifice

I am utterly serious in my wish to die for God; do not put any obstacles in my way. Let me be a meal for the beasts in the arena, so they will open for me the way to God. I am God's wheat; and the lions' teeth will grind me into the purest flour, to make bread for God. Let those creatures be my tomb; let them eat every scrap of my flesh, so there is nothing to be cleared away. When there is no trace of my body for the world to see, then I shall truly be Christ's disciple. So pray to God for me, that the lions may be the instruments by which I am made into a sacrifice to God.

For the present the chains around my body are educating me to relinquish all earthly desires. As I am taken by land and sea from Syria to Rome, the soldiers to whom I am bound grow more insolent each day – and their insolence teaches me humility. When I face the lions, I shall feel relieved. All I pray is that they may be swift in their work. I shall invite them to attack me, so they might devour me quickly; and, if they are still reluctant, I shall compel them. Please forgive me my yearning for a martyr's death; you must trust me to know what is best for myself. This is the first stage of my discipleship; no power, visible or invisible, can grudge me my coming to Jesus Christ.

All the wealth on earth, and all the kingdoms of every continent, would mean nothing to me. Dying in Christ is better than being emperor of the entire world.

Ignatius of Antioch: Romans 4, 5, 6

An anvil under a hammer

There are some amongst you who distort the teachings of
Christ for their own ends. Do not let them disturb or upset
you. Stand firmly, like an anvil under the hammer. The mark
of a true champion is to stand up to punishment, and still
emerge victorious. It is the duty of every Christian to con-
front any challenge or trial in God's cause.

Take care that widows within the community are not
neglected; be their guardian, on God's behalf. Do nothing
without first consulting God. Gather the community frequently, in order to worship God. Do not be overbearing in
your manner towards slaves, whether men or women; urge
them to be better slaves, in order to win honour before God.
Assure them that they will gain their freedom in heaven; but
tell them that the church lacks the funds to purchase their
freedom on earth.

Tell the sisters in the community to be content, both
physically and emotionally, with their husbands; and tell the
brothers to love their wives as the Lord loves the church.
Those who are capable of remaining celibate throughout their
lives, should not marry; but equally they should not boast of
their restraint, for boasting would destroy its value. When a
man and woman wish to marry, they should seek their
leader's advice, that he may judge whether they are compat-
ible in spirit.

The honour of God should the aim of everything that
people do.

Ignatius of Antioch: Polycarp 3, 4, 5

From the earliest decades, as it encountered Greek philosophy, Christianity had to reflect on itself with intellectual rigour.

Justin (d. c. 155), a respected philosopher, defended Christianity against its external detractors. Irenaeus (d. c. 173), bishop of Lyons in France, defended Christianity from internal corruption. Origen (d. 253), living in Alexandria, engaged in daring theological speculations.

Basil of Caesarea (d. 379) pioneered monastic life, forming communities on his family estate. John Chrysostom (d. 407), patriarch of Constantinople, was forced into exile for his strictures on the wealthy. Augustine of Hippo (d. 430) developed the first comprehensive Christian theology. Leo (d. 461), a pope in Rome, composed a statement on the relationship of God and Christ, which was widely accepted.

Anselm (d. 1109), archbishop of Canterbury, wrote a famous proof of the existence of God. Another monk, Bernard of Clairvaux (d. 1153), developed a theology of mysticism. Thomas Aquinas (d. 1274) also sought to prove God's existence. Eckhart (d. 1327) followed Bernard in developing a mystical theology. Martin Luther (d. 1546) in Germany and John Calvin (d. 1564) in Geneva were the main leaders of the Protestant reformation, providing its theological foundation. Jacobus Arminius (d. 1609), a Protestant pastor in Holland, explored the connection between human freedom and divine providence. Blaise Pascal (d. 1662) and Friedrich Schleiermacher (d. 1834) tried to reinterpret Christian theology in an age of growing scepticism.

The judgement of reason

Reason requires that philosophers should honour and cherish only the truth; they should not merely accept old opinions, if these are shown to be worthless. Reason does not merely require us to avoid bad behaviour and reject false ideas; those of us who love the truth, must on every occasion do and say what is right – even at the cost of our own lives.

You, my accusers, are known to be pious guardians of justice, and wise lovers of truth. By giving us a fair hearing you will prove your piety and wisdom. I do not try to flatter you; nor do I want to win your favour with eloquence. I ask you to judge my words according to the strict and precise application of reason. Do not be moved by prejudice or superstition, or by evil rumours; to be influenced by these things would be a betrayal of yourselves. We for our part are convinced that no harm can come to us, unless we are guilty of some kind of evil or crime.

The mere ascription of a name to a group of people implies nothing about their moral standing; what matters is the behaviour associated with that name. We are charged with being Christian. To us that name is gracious. But we do not ask to be pardoned on account of a name. If our conduct is blameless, then any punishment would be unjust.

Justin 2, 4

Atheism and belief

We are accused of being atheist. We certainly admit to being atheist with regard to the false gods which many people worship. But we are not atheist with regard to the true God, the Father of righteousness, self-control and all other virtues – the God who is untouched by evil. Nor are we atheist with regard to the Son, who came from the Father, and taught us about the Father. Nor are we atheist with regard to the prophetic Spirit, who guides our thoughts towards the truth, and who transmits the truth to others.

We yearn for the life which is eternal and pure; we strive to dwell with God, who created and fashioned all things. We are eager to proclaim our faith to others. And we are certain in our belief that those who follow God in their actions, shall indeed go to heaven.

When you hear that we are looking for a kingdom, you rashly presume that we mean a human kingdom. But we speak of God's kingdom. This is why we are happy to proclaim our faith when we come to trial – even though death is the penalty. If we were looking for a human kingdom, we should deny our faith in order to save our lives; or at least we should try to keep our faith secret. But our faith is not connected with the present political order; so we are not troubled at the prospect of death. Besides, we must all die some time!

Justin 6, 8, 11

Occupying one house

Although the church is now spreading throughout the world to the ends of the earth, it has a single faith, which it received from the apostles. It believes in one Jesus Christ, the Son of God, who became flesh for our salvation; and in the Holy Spirit, who preached through the prophets, and now preaches through the disciples of Jesus.

Thus, despite the great distances between groups of believers, it seems as if they occupy one house. Their common faith draws them together in heart and soul. They speak the same words, and they proclaim the same message. There are many different languages in the world; but one Christian faith is conveyed in them all. Thus, the church in Germany believes and proclaims exactly the same message as do the Spanish and the Celtic churches; and this message is also preached in Jerusalem, which is the centre of the world.

Just as the sun, which was created by God, is the same throughout the world, so the same truth now shines in every nation, and enlightens all those who respond to it in a spirit of faith. Those who are eloquent speakers, cannot add to the truth; and those who are stumbling speakers, cannot diminish the truth. Since truth is one and the same, regardless of who expresses it, no one can improve on it or undermine it.

Irenaeus: Against Heresies 1.10

The son of humanity

The Word of God became a human being, in order that men and women may become sons and daughters of God.

In no other way could we have become pure and immortal. How could human flesh become pure and immortal, unless purity and immortality had become flesh? Only by this means could our impurity be absorbed by purity, and our own mortality be absorbed by immortality.

Thus, the Son of God, who is our Lord, is also the son of humanity. This same Lord has become the first-fruits of the resurrection of humanity, enabling all human beings to rise to life. He is the head, and we are his body; and together we become immortal.

God's mercy is wonderfully abundant. When he sees people sin, he plans their salvation; he enables them to become joined to the Son, and thereby share in the Son's victory over death.

Irenaeus:
Against Heresies 3.19

The agent of creation

Through the creation the Word of God reveals the Creator. Through the world the Word reveals the one who is the architect of the world. Through the infinite beauty of the world's design the Word reveals the one who conceived beauty. Thus the Word, who is the Son, reveals the Father. All creatures, by their very existence, testify to the power and wisdom of God; but not every creature believes in God.

The Word has expressed himself in the words of many prophets; and in this way he has proclaimed the Father. Everyone has heard the words of prophets, but not all have believed. The same Word became visible and tangible in Jesus Christ. Thus, all who encounter Jesus, also encounter the Father; but not everyone believes.

The Word, who is the Son, was the divine agent of creation from the beginning. And the Word reveals God to everyone, because that is what the Father wishes.

Irenaeus: Against Heresies 4.6

Transformed in God's image

There is one God, who by his Word and through his wisdom created and ordered all things. In these final times God's Word became a human being, to live among human beings, in the person of Jesus Christ, in order to reconcile humanity with God. The prophets of the past proclaimed the Word in words; now the Word has mingled with human flesh, thereby uniting God and humanity.

I acknowledge that no human being can see the stupendous glory of God, and live; in himself God is beyond comprehension. Yet every human being can experience the love, the kindness, the mercy and the power of God. All who turn to God in love, receive his love – as the prophets have always testified. Human beings can never attain true and lasting joy by their own efforts; but through God this is possible. Human beings cannot perceive God through their own powers; but by his own choice God has revealed himself to humanity.

God the Son appeared in human flesh, and now he manifests himself by his Spirit – when he wishes, to whom he wishes, and as he wishes. Those who encounter God's self-revelation, and respond by putting their whole trust in him, become his sons and daughters. The Spirit transforms them in the image of God the Son, that in the fullness of time they may enjoy eternal life in the presence of God the Father. God's sons and daughters see the light, and live in the light – and they reflect its splendour.

Irenaeus: Against Heresies 4.20

The Word as the agent of creation

God's Word sustains the universe in being. His nature and his greatness cannot be seen or described by any of the creatures he has made. Yet he is known to all of them. The Word conveys to all that there is one God the Father, who brings all things into being and sustains them in being. Only the Word, who is the Son, has seen the Father; and it is through the Word that we know the Father.

The Son has revealed the Father from the beginning, because he was with the Father from the beginning. At appropriate times he gave to humanity prophetic visons and spiritual gifts of all kinds; then he came in the flesh to serve humanity directly. The Son reveals the Father in an orderly manner, at opportune times, when humanity can derive the greatest benefit; and where there is order, there is harmony.

Thus, the Word is the dispenser of the Father's grace to humanity; and he never fails to be generous. He has revealed God to humanity, and thereby raised humanity to God. He shields the Father from human sight, so that human beings will never undervalue God through familiarity, but will always have to reach out to God. Yet he reveals God to humanity in so many ways that human beings have no cause for ignoring God.

God's glory is most fully revealed when ordinary human beings are transformed in the image of his Son.

Irenaeus: *Against Heresies* 4.20

Being made holy

We derive our existence from God the Father; we derive our rationality from God the Son; and we derive our sanctity from the Holy Spirit. We become holy through our participation in the Spirit. And when we have been sanctified through the Holy Spirit, we are capable of receiving the Son – of being transformed in the image of Jesus Christ, and sharing his knowledge and wisdom.

In giving us our existence, the Father's purpose is that we should make this progress; he wants us to move from our present level of existence to the highest level. The Holy Spirit cleanses and purifies us, making us ready to acquire divine knowledge and wisdom. When all the stains of corruption and ignorance have been washed away, we are worthy of God – worthy to be embraced by him as his sons and daughters.

Origen: On First Principles 1.3

The coherence of the world

Although the world has many different species and types of objects, it is not incoherent or disorderly. A human body consists of many different organs, but they are held together by one soul. In the same way the world is like some immense living being which is united by a single soul – namely, the power and reason of God. There is great diversity in the motives and purposes of all the creatures in the world. Yet taken together these motives and purposes have a single end – namely, the fulfilment of God's plan for the world.

Thus, we may say that every species in the world exists because God wishes it to exist; that the qualities every species possesses, are qualities which God has imposed upon it; and that the natural instincts of every species have been implanted by God in accordance with his plan. Anyone who claims that the different species in the world have come about by accident, through some random process, is challenging the very existence of God.

Origen: On First Principles 2.1

The God-human

It cannot be doubted that the soul of Jesus Christ was the same in nature as all souls. But whereas other souls have the capacity to choose good and evil, the soul belonging to Christ chose only goodness, and was bound to goodness in such a manner that it could not be separated from it. Thus, in choosing goodness, it became goodness. Thus, Christ had a human soul, but was incapable of sin.

If a lump of iron is put into a fire, and is left there, it receives heat in all its pores and veins, and becomes wholly fire. In the same way the soul of Jesus was always in the Word of God, and thus became God in all that it did, felt and knew.

Therefore the soul of Jesus was the link connecting God with human flesh; without such a link it would be impossible for God to mingle with human flesh. In this sense Jesus was a God-human; he was the Word of God made flesh.

Origen: On First Principles 2.6

Restoration to unity

In the final consummation evil itself will not be destroyed, because evil was created by God. But the hostile purpose of evil will perish, because this does not come from God. Thus, evil will cease to be an enemy, and will cease to destroy people's souls. Nothing is impossible to the omnipotence of God; there is nothing that cannot be healed by the Father. He made all things that they might exist; and if things were made to exist they cannot become non-existent.

At the final consummation all things will be restored to unity. But this should not be imagined as a sudden event; rather it should be envisaged as a very gradual process, passing through countless ages. Little by little each individual will be corrected and purified. Some will lead the way, making rapid progress to the height of perfection; some will be just behind them; and others will be far behind. Multitudes of people and groups, who were once enemies of God, will be reconciled to him.

Origen: On First Principles 3.6

The value of evil

We commonly say that within God's providence all things in the world are valuable and nothing is useless. But let us develop that assertion more clearly. God does not prevent evil when it is enacted by human beings, although he has the power to do so. But he uses evil, and those who enact it, for his purposes. By means of the evil actions he displays the glory of righteous actions; virtue, if not opposed by vice, would not shine.

More particularly, if the wickedness of Judas were removed and his treachery annulled, the cross of Jesus would also be removed. And if Jesus Christ had not been crucified, then he could not have risen to life, thereby winning victory over death. And if he had not defeated death, we should have no hope of immortality.

Consider evil itself. If there were no evil, we should not have the opportunity to struggle against it. And if we had no struggle against evil, we could not be victorious – and thus we should not deserve to share Christ's risen life.

Origen: Homily on Numbers 14.2

Transforming the soul

We know that every soul has the same nature; and we assert that no nature was made evil by the one who created the universe. Thus, people become wicked through the influence of their parents, through corrupt activities or through the influence of their environment; wickedness is acquired, and not innate.

We also assert that God's Word is capable of converting people from wickedness back to goodness. Indeed, he is not only capable of this, but it is quite easy for him – if people entrust themselves to him, and commit themselves to act in ways that are pleasing to him. But if some people find this hard, we must presume that the reason lies in their refusal to accept God as the ruler of the universe, and as the just judge of all actions. Our point is that those who accept God's rule, and who make a clear choice to submit to that rule, find that God's Word begins to transform them quite swiftly and readily.

Being transformed by God's Word is like walking on a tightrope. It seems horribly difficult to spectators who have never attempted it. But when people seriously attempt it, and practise day by day, they are surprised how easily they learn.

Origen: Against Celsus 3.69

Despoiling creation

God is concerned not just with his creation as a whole, but
with every living creature individually. It is true that his care
for the whole never fails. Thus, if the whole creation deteri-
orates through the activities of particular creatures, God takes
corrective measures, bringing the whole back to himself. In
the case of animals and insects he is never angry, because
their misbehaviour is irrational. But human beings are
rational; so if human beings despoil his creation in any way,
he rebukes and punishes them. It is the purpose of all creatures, rational and irrational, to play their part in fulfilling
God's purpose.

Origen: Against Celsus 4.99

God's providence and will

It is our fixed and unchangeable belief that God is incorporeal, omnipotent and invisible; and that at the same time he cares for our mortal lives, and that nothing takes place in heaven or on earth outside his providence. But note that we have said 'outside his providence', not 'outside his will'. Many things take place outside God's will; but nothing takes place outside his providence.

Providence is the process by which God administers, orders and watches over events as they happen. His will is the process by which he decides what should and should not happen. Our belief in God's providence implies that we believe he reveals his will, showing human beings how they should behave. If he did not reveal his will, he would be lacking in care and love for human beings; by revealing his will, he expresses his love.

Origen: Homily on Genesis 3.2

Preparing to know God

You must strive for a quiet mind. If the eyes are perpetually restless, they cannot appreciate a beautiful object set before them; they glance this way and that, and so fail to discern the subtlety of the object's form and colour. Equally if the mind is perpetually restless, distracted by a thousand worldly concerns, it cannot apprehend the truth.

You cannot write on a wax tablet, without first erasing the marks already on it. Equally your mind cannot receive divine truth, without first unlearning the false notions and prejudices that you have acquired in the past.

Solitude is the best context for quietening the mind and unlearning falsehood. Seek out a place of solitude, where you can train your soul without interruption, nourishing your soul with thoughts of God. Begin each day like a choir of angels, honouring God with songs of praise. As the day brightens, pursue your various tasks to the accompaniment of prayers, and season your labour with the salt of more songs. A pleasant melody composes the mind and calms its passions.

Gradually your tongue will lose its appetite for idle conversation, your eyes will cease to crave stimulation, and your ears will no longer hunger for gossip. This will enable your mind to turn inwards and begin its ascent to the contemplation of God.

Basil of Caesarea: Letters 2

The limitations of language

The nature and majesty of God can neither be defined by human language nor comprehended by human intellect. It cannot be explained or grasped by formulae or concepts. In speaking about God we find ourselves compelled to use images and metaphors. In order to see God face to face, we should have first to be made perfect in mind and soul. But in our present state we can only perceive God indirectly and partially – as if we were seeing a reflection in a darkened mirror. So let us cherish these perceptions with joy, while we wait patiently for perfection in time to come.

When we study our sacred texts, we are made more and more aware of the partiality of our present knowledge, and of our inability to pierce the mystery of God. As we make progress in the spiritual life, we become more and more aware of the distance we have still to travel. No single word or title is sufficient to signify the glorious nature of God. One person uses the term 'God', but this does not denote his fatherly love for us; another person uses 'Father', but this does not denote his creative power. And what term can convey his goodness, wisdom and countless other attributes? Indeed, all words and titles for God are no more than human inventions, trying to relate God to some human experience.

Basil of Caesarea: Concerning Faith 3

The simplicity and complexity of God's Spirit

The Holy Spirit is generous in bestowing gifts; and every creature can be made holy by the power of the Spirit. Those who wish to live virtuously, reach out to the Spirit; and as the breath of the Spirit blows through their souls, they are carried up towards God. The Spirit lacks nothing, because the Spirit is the source of all perfection. The Spirit does not need to rise to life, because the Spirit is the supplier of life. The Spirit requires no additions, because from all eternity the Spirit is abundantly full. The Spirit is our source of divine knowledge, enlightening our minds in our search for truth.

Although the Spirit is by its nature inaccessible, yet through the generosity of God we can receive the Spirit. The Spirit fills all creation with its power; yet this power can only be apprehended by those worthy to do so. The Spirit is simple in essence, but complex in its effects. The Spirit is present in its fullness in each individual, but also present in its fullness in all people. The Spirit is shared, but cannot be divided.

The Spirit is like the beam of the sun. You enjoy the sun as if it were beaming for you alone; yet in reality the sun is beaming everywhere. In the same way you receive the Spirit as if the Spirit had come uniquely to you; yet in reality the Spirit comes to everyone.

Through the Spirit hearts are raised high, the weak are made strong and those aspiring for perfection become holy.

Basil of Caesarea: On the Holy Spirit 9

The seed of love

You cannot teach someone to love God, any more than you can teach someone to appreciate beauty or to cherish life. No one taught us to love our parents, or whoever brought us up. Similarly, and more emphatically, we do not learn to love God through a course of instruction. We love God because the seed of love has been sown in every human being. Those who have been enrolled in the school of God's love are those who acknowledge and rejoice in this seed, cultivating it with acts of charity, nurturing it with meditation and in every way fostering its growth.

Thus, the commandment that we should love God is like water on the seed of love. The proof of this is not external; we can discover the proof by looking inside ourselves. We naturally desire beautiful things, although we differ as to what we regard as beautiful. And without being taught, we naturally have affection towards our relatives and close friends, and we feel gratitude towards those who show us kindness. What is more beautiful than the beauty of God? What is more captivating than the glory of God? What desire in the soul is keener and sharper than the desire to be close to God? What gratitude is fuller than our gratitude to God for all his blessings?

Basil of Caesarea: The Longer Rule 2

God's greatest work of creation

Even a lifetime is too short to describe the richness and diversity of God's creation. So we shall pass over in silence the rising of the sun, the circuits of the moon, the patterns of the seasons, the falling of rain, the gushing of springs, the surging sea, the plants and trees that cover the earth, the birds of the air, the animals on land, the fish in the ocean – we shall pass over all that gives us pleasure and nourishment. This allows us to concentrate on God's greatest work on earth: the fashioning of human beings. It is impossible to be silent about the glory of humanity; yet no single human being is worthy to speak of it.

God made human beings in his image and likeness; he gave human beings the capacity for knowledge of him; he equipped human beings with intelligence and reason above that of all other creatures; and he gave human beings the responsibility to care for the rest of his creation. When human beings sin, God does not abandon them; on the contrary, he sends prophets and teachers to rebuke and guide them. He stirs up in human beings a love of virtue; and he inspires some to become saints, in order to be an example to the others. Finally he gives human beings Jesus Christ, who saves them from death, and shows them the way to eternal life.

God asks for nothing in return. He is content merely to be loved.

Basil of Caesarea: The Longer Rule 2

The seal of God

You cannot succeed in loving God or your neighbour, as God commands, if your mind is perpetually distracted.

You cannot learn any art of science, if you are constantly flitting from one subject to another. You cannot master any craft or skill if you are not prepared to persevere. Your activities must correspond with the ends you wish to achieve, since nothing is achieved by inappropriate methods. You cannot become an expert blacksmith, if you insist on practising pottery; you will not obtain an athlete's wreath by practising the flute! For each end a proper and necessary effort is required.

Thus, you must practise the art of pleasing God, in the manner prescribed in Christ's gospel. This requires you to disengage your mind from trivial preoccupations, and to attend to God. To follow God you must break free from the chains that bind you to this world; you must break every kind of worldly habit. Unless you renounce every kind of obsession with the body and its desires, you will never succeed in pleasing God. You must train your mind to a new pattern of thinking.

When you have done this you must remain vigilant, to ensure that you never slide away from God again. Constantly fill your mind with thoughts of his glory; and do not allow your imagination to lure your mind away from God. Let God print himself on your mind like an indelible seal.

Basil of Caesarea: The Longer Rule 5

Mutual dependence

Living in community is more natural, and more likely to prove spiritually valuable, than living in solitude. None of us is self-sufficient. We depend on one another for the material necessities of life. Indeed, the body itself is an image of our mutual dependence. The foot, for example, may be able to do certain things by itself; but separated from the rest of our bodies its activities would be useless, and it would soon wither and die.

Those who live permanently in solitude, may be likened to feet divorced from the body. Their efforts are useless to anyone apart from themselves; and they are liable to wither in both body and spirit. God, in creating human beings, ordained that they should need one another; he bound them together.

How can you grow in humiilty, if there is no one against whom you can compare yourself? How can you express compassion, when there is no one to evoke that noble feeling? How can you understand and interpret the teachings of Jesus, without discussing those teachings with others?

Living in community is like life in the arena: you are continuously stretched to perform better.

Basil of Caesarea: The Longer Rule 7

Harmonious relationships

You should be patient, whatever trials you have to endure. Although you have the right to rebuke a person who has wronged you, you must not do this out of anger for having been wronged; your only concern should be to teach the wrongdoer the ways of God.

You should not say anything against an absent person, even if your words are true. You should turn away from anyone who is speaking against an absent person. You should never indulge in idle talk, which is useless to the listener and offensive to God. Nor should you deliver speeches of exhortation, unless your listeners have given you authority to do so.

Apply yourself quietly to your proper tasks. Do not seek to be honoured by others; and do not regard yourself as more worthy of honour than anyone else. Be generous in conferring honour on others. Only leave your proper task if someone urgently needs your help.

Congratulate others for what they do well. Do not hold grudges against those who have wronged you and repented; forgiveness should be total. When you find that others dislike you, heal the rift with special acts of kindness. When you find you have done something wrong, do not hesitate; make amends at once.

Basil of Caesarea: The Shorter Rule

Churches and the poor

You should become discerning Christians, learning to honour Christ in ways of which he approves. When someone is honoured, the form of honour should be appropriate to the person receiving it, not to the person bestowing it. God wants you to honour Christ by giving generously to the poor. God does not need you to give golden chalices to churches; but he does want you to have a golden heart.

Of course, it is quite permissible to donate golden chalices and other precious objects, in order to beautify churches; but there is no substitute for giving to the poor. The Lord will not refuse the gift of a precious object, but he prefers practical generosity to those in need. In the case of a gift to a church, only the donor benefits; but in the case of a gift to the poor, both the donor and the recipient benefit. The gift of a golden chalice may be extravagant in generosity; but a gift to the poor is an expression of love.

What is the point of weighing down Christ's table with golden chalices, while he himself is starving – for he is in every starving man, woman and child? Will you fashion a cup of gold, and yet withhold a cup of water from a thirsty mouth? What is the use of silken hangings round Christ's table, if Christ lacks a coat for his back? Beautify God's house, if that is what you want to do, but never neglect your brother and sister in need; they are temples of infinitely greater value.

John Chrysostom: On Matthew's Gospel, Sermon 50

Sharing the faith

There is nothing so cold as Christians who do not want to share their faith with others. Humble birth is no excuse for not proclaiming your faith; the apostles were of humble birth. Lack of education is no excuse; the apostles were illiterate. Sickness is no excuse; the apostles were frequently sick. All Christians are capable of speaking to their neighbours about their faith.

Look at the trees of the forest. See how sturdy, beautiful and tall they are, and how smooth is their bark; yet they do not bear fruit. So in your garden you prefer to plant pomegranates and olive trees; they are not so fine in appearance as the trees of the forest, but they bear fruit. There are many Christians who devote themselves to studying theology, and yet who never urge others to devote themselves to Christ; they are like the trees of the forest.

In the natural world, plants grow and animals behave according to their nature. It is the nature of being a Christian to pass on the joy of faith to all who will listen. Do not insult God by keeping your faith to yourself. To claim that the sun cannot shine would be an insult to God; it is an even greater insult that Christians have nothing to give.

John Chrysostom: On Acts, Sermon 4

Hard hearts

God gave his Son to humanity. So why do you refuse to give a single morsel of bread to those in need? For your sake God allowed his Son Jesus Christ to suffer the most terrible agony. Yet when you turn away the starving from your door, you show your contempt for Christ. If you were to give generously to those in need, you would be drawing on an account which Christ himself has put it credit; and your action would earn you further interest. For your sake Christ was delivered into the hands of his enemies, and murdered; and prior to that, as he wandered from place to place, preaching and healing, he had no home, and he was frequently hungry. Yet you only give something to another person, in order to receive some greater benefit in return – and even then you show great caution.

How senseless you are! How hard you are – as hard as flint! Despite all the encouragement which you have received, you remained locked in the prison of your own heartless cruelty. When you think of Christ, why do you not take pity on his poverty; why do you not feel compassion for his suffering? And why do feelings of pity and compassion not stir you to acts of charity? You are not being asked to go hungry yourself; you are only being asked to share a little of your abundance with those who have nothing.

John Chrysostom: On Romans, Sermon 15

Giving gladly

It is not enough simply to give to the poor; you must give without grumbling. It is not even enough to give without grumbling; you must give with a glad and willing heart.

When you help the poor, two attitudes should always be manifest: generosity and joy. Why do you moan about the duty to give to the poor? Why do you express such resentment at having to share your wealth with those in need? If you resist giving to the poor, you are showing no mercy; you are simply exposing your callousness and lack of compassion. If you are full of resentment, how can you help someone in the depths of misery?

In fact, giving to others in a spirit of resentment only demeans and humiliates them, because it makes them feel beholden to you. But if you give to others in a spirit of joy, you create no sense of debt, because the receiver can see that you too are benefiting from your gift. A donor's resentment depresses the spirit of the receiver; a donor's joy uplifts the receiver's spirit. If you give gladly, even if the gift is small, it will be munificent. If you give resentfully, even if the gift is substantial, it will be a pittance.

John Chrysostom: On Romans, Sermon 21

Peasants as philosophers

The cross of Jesus convicted the world of sin; and, through
the efforts of largely uneducated people, the cross drew the
world to itself. These uneducated people succeeded not by
eloquence, but by the sincerity of their faith; they spoke from
personal experience about God, about true religion and about
the right way to live. They were illiterate peasants; but they
had the insights of philosophers. They demonstrated how the
foolishness of God is wiser than human wisdom.

They also demonstrated how the weakness of God is
stronger than human strength. The cross of Jesus symbolizes
the weakness of God; yet, through the efforts of these uneducated people, the cross turned the world upside down. As
the secular authorities tried the suppress the name of the one
who was crucified, the cross gripped people's hearts and
minds. Indeed, the persecution of Christianity actually pro-
moted it, causing it to flourish and grow – while the religion
espoused by its persecutors withered and died. Jesus died
powerless; yet he overcame the most powerful empire in the
world.

John Chrysostom: On 1 Corinthians, Sermon 4

Love and obedience in marriage

There is no relationship so intimate as that between husband and wife – if they are united as they should be. How much mutual obedience is required in a marriage! How much love is also required!

Do you want your spouse to obey you, as disciples should obey Christ? Then you should love your spouse as much as Christ loves his disciples. If it were necessary for you to die in order to save your spouse, you should not hesitate. If it were necessary to suffer the most terrible agony in order to spare your spouse pain, you should not hesitate. Indeed, any suffering that you may endure for the sake of your spouse, is nothing compared with the suffering that Christ endured for your sake. Indeed, when you suffer for your spouse, you are suffering for someone with whom you are already united; whereas Christ suffered for the sake of those who hated and opposed him.

Christ wooed his enemies with unwavering love and tenderness, and many are now his friends; woo your spouse in the same manner. Even if you think your spouse despises you, cherish your spouse as Christ cherishes his disciples. Even if your spouse constantly humiliates you, retain your dignity by being kind and considerate in return.

John Chrysostom: On Ephesians, Sermon 20

Informing the conscience

You should constantly strive to inform your conscience. You should do this by reviewing your actions, asking whether any deserve correction or punishment. You are naturally indignant when someone commits serious sins and escapes with impunity; but it is far better to be indignant at your own sins. Moreover, you should not assess a sin by the action itself, but by the attitude behind the action; and you are only capable of assessing accurately your own attitudes – other people's attitudes are a matter for them to assess.

For example, stealing may seem worse than fraud; yet the attitude behind both is greed, so both are equally bad. It may seem worse to steal gold than silver; but, again, both have the same root within the mind. A person who steals a small object will not hesitate at the chance of stealing a large object. A poor person who robs a poorer person would not hesitate to rob the rich, if the opportunity arose.

You may complain that your ruler is stealing from his subjects through excessive taxes. But do you never take what does not belong to you? It is no use objecting that he takes vast sums, while you take only a little; the attitude behind both actions is the same. The Lord makes no distinction between the small gift of a poor person and the large gift of a rich person; equally he makes no distinction between the small sins of a weak person and the large sins of a powerful person.

John Chrysostom: On 1 Timothy, Sermon 3

Celebrating creation

God made this world beautiful, glorious, varied and abundant. He has given it the capacity to meet your every need; it nourishes your body, and also uplifts your soul by leading you towards knowledge of himself. For your sake he has made the sky radiant with stars, and adorned it with the moon at night and the sun by day.

Everything in this world has been fashioned to give you joy. In every corner of the earth trees are growing. It is impossible to know all the different species. You can simply marvel at the varied fruit, fragrances, barks and leaves; and you can rejoice in the healing properties that many of the trees possess.

God has made all these trees for your sake. And for your sake God has inspired you to build cities, and to fill them with works of art. He has prompted you to build roads out of the cities, so you can enjoy the countryside. He has given you the ability to sleep, so you can refresh your body and mind. And, above all, he has given you life, so that you can appreciate the magnificence of his creation. The world will still exist for you when you awake tomorrow – and by then it will be even better!

The providence of God shines in every object and in every creature in the world. Do not try to scrutinize God's motives in acting so generously towards you; the thoughts of God are impossible to fathom. All you need to know is that world has been given to you out of pure love. God requires nothing in return – except gratitude.

John Chrysostom: On Providence 7

Unity in adversity

Christ is with me; so my persecutors do not frighten me. Let the waves of their anger rise up against me; they are no more than cobwebs to me. If my loving congregation had not held me back, I should have gone into exile this very day. I say constantly to myself: 'May the Lord's will be done.' I have no interest in what this person or that person wishes; I want only to know what God wishes. God's will is my fortress, my immoveable rock, my sturdy staff. If God wishes something to be, then so be it. If God wishes me to be here, then here I shall stay. Wherever he wishes me to be, I thank him.

Wherever I am, there in spirit is my congregation also; and wherever my congregation is, there I am also. My congregation and I are one body. Just as the body cannot be separated from the head, and the head cannot be separated from the body, I cannot be separated from my people. We may be separated by space, but we are united by love. Not even death can sever us; even if my body dies, my soul will survive – and my soul will remember my people.

My congregation is my family; its members are my parents, my brother and sisters, and my children. They are dearer to me than light; the rays of the sun are dark compared with the rays of their love. Indeed, their love is weaving for me a crown that I shall wear for all eternity.

John Chrysostom: Before Exile

The restless heart

To praise you, Lord, is the deepest desire of a human being. You stir people to take pleasure in praising you, because you have created them for yourself. The human heart is restless, until it rests in you.

Who will enable me to find rest in you? Who can help me to receive you into my heart? Who can intoxicate my heart with your love, so that I can forget all the wrongs I have done, and embrace you, the only source of goodness.

What are you to me? Help me to find the right words with which to express myself to you. What am I to you? You command me to love you; and, if I fail to love you, then you are angry with me, and threaten me with terrible suffering. If I do not love you, what harm does that do?

In your mercy, Lord, tell me what you are to me. Say to me that you are my salvation. Speak to me, that I may hear. The ears of my heart are open to you, Lord. After you have spoken, I shall run to you, and cling to you.

Do not hide your face from me. Let me die, if that is the only way I can see you. The house of my soul is too small for you to enter; enlarge it, that you may enter.

Augustine of Hippo: Confessions 1

The objects of spiritual love

What do I love, when I love God? Not material or temporal beauty; not some brilliant light that dazzles my eyes; not some sweet melody that captivated my ears; not the fragrance of flowers or perfume; not henna or honey; not a body that arouses sexual desire. It is not any of these that I love, when I love God.

And yet, when I love God, I do indeed love a certain kind of beauty, a certain kind of voice, a certain fragrance and a certain embrace. But these come not from outside myself; they come from within. My soul is bathed in a light that is not bounded by space; it listens to a sound that never dies away; it breathes a fragrance that is not carried away on the wind; it tastes food that is not consumed by eating; it enjoys an embrace which fulfils every desire, and which never ends. That is what I love, when I love God.

Augustine of Hippo:
Confessions 10

The direction of love

What is love? Can love ever induce you to harm other people? Does love merely imply refraining from evil, or does it imply actively doing good? Does love make you do everything in your power for the object of your love? Is it possible to love and pray for your enemies? When the needs of a friend and an enemy conflict, does love require you to help the friend or the enemy? What is the connection between faith and love?

Let love be constrained by faith. Love is never idle; and all actions, good and evil alike, are motivated by love. People become thieves, because they love material objects. People commit adultery, because they love sexual adventure. People commit murder, because they love violence. Every kind of wickedness is the expression of some form of love.

The purpose of faith is to purify love. The waters of love naturally pour down into the gutter; faith diverts the waters into the garden. Without faith people pour their love into the world; with faith they pour it towards the one who created the world.

Am I telling you to give up loving? Not at all! If you love nothing, you will become lazy and listless; you will die even while you live. Love with fervour; but direct your love with care.

Augustine of Hippo: Commentary on Psalm 31

Friendship with all people

Brothers and sisters, I beg you to show charity not only to one another, but also to those who are not Christian, and to Christians who hold different beliefs to your own. Love them as if they held the same beliefs that you do. Seek them out, and make friends with them. They may ask: 'Why do you come to us? What do you want with us?' Say to them in reply: 'We come to you because you are our brothers and sisters; and we want to befriend you.' They may say: 'Go away! We have nothing in common with you.' You should reply: 'We have something very important in common with you: God is our Father, and he is your Father. Therefore we should be united as brothers and sisters.'

Remember how the milk of Christ's love helped you to grow in faith, when you first became Christian. Remember how the bread of Christ's love continues to fortify you. Do not try to deny others that same milk and bread. If they respond to you with animosity, remember that their animosity is superficial; within their hearts they are weak and vulnerable. Thus, I am appealing to you on behalf of the weak; I am appealing to you on behalf of those whose attitudes may be crude and distorted, but who are still your spiritual siblings.

Augustine of Hippo: Commentary on Psalm 32

The prosperity of the wicked

You are troubled by seeing evil people prosper. They enjoy abundant wealth and robust health; they occupy positions of high rank, and they seem utterly secure. You observe the happiness of their families, the respect in which they are held by their neighbours, and the influence they exert in political and social affairs; their lives seem unmarred by sadness. You also observe their moral and spiritual bankruptcy. And you are inclined to conclude that divine judgement does not exist – that everything is governed by chance.

Your error lies in your conception of time. You think that the prosperity of evil people lasts a long time; but in God's eyes an entire lifespan is short. Abandon yourself to God, and time will shorten for you as well. These evil people live only on the surface of existence, and do not strike deep roots. They may be green through the winter; but, when the summer sun starts to shine, they wither away. Now is the season of winter, and your glory is not yet apparent. But when the winter frosts cease, and the summer comes, your leaves will burst forth – and will remain green even when the sun is at its hottest. This is because your roots go deep, drawing nourishment from the depths of God's love.

When will your spring arrive? When will green leaves cover your nakedness? When will you bear fruit? You must wait patiently, trusting in the Lord; and in the meantime you should take every opportunity to do good.

Augustine of Hippo: Commentary on Psalm 36

Moral madness

Some people's strength is based not on wealth, nor in their physical well-being, nor in their position in society, but in a sense of their own righteousness. You should guard yourself, above all others, against such people. You should avoid their company, and you should suppress any temptation to imitate them. People whose pride is based on wealth, physical prowess or status, are manifestly foolish, because wealth, prowess and status are temporal, fleeting, unreliable and ephemeral. But righteousness is permanent and solid; and those believing in their own righteousness can appear wise.

'I am strong,' such people declare, 'so I do not need a doctor.' But their strength is not healthy; it stems from a moral madness. Nothing is stronger than those who are mad; they can intimidate even the strongest of sane people. Yet madness leads to its own destruction. So I urge those who believe in their own righteousness, to seek help – to seek Christ, who can cure them.

Christ is the great exemplar of humility. He has shown us how to be humble; he even allowed himself to be baptized by one of his servants. And he teaches us that, by acknowledging our own weakness, we find strength in God.

Augustine of Hippo: Commentary on Psalm 58

Constant change

Our years slip away from us day by day. Past years no longer exist and future years will soon pass into oblivion. This moment, this very moment at which you are absorbing these words, is all that exists. The first hours of the day have already passed, the remainder of the day will soon pass into oblivion.

Nothing that exists remains constant. Every human body is subject to a continual process of change; it has no permanence. It ages; it is altered by external circumstances and it is affected by illness and accident. No part of the body is constant. Even the stars have no constancy; their pattern is subtly changing with every moment, as they hurtle through space – even though we cannot always discern the changes. Nothing rests; nothing stays the same.

Nor is the human mind any more constant. Consider how many thoughts and distractions assail it. Consider how the body's various desires wreak havoc inside it. The human mind is said to be rational. Yet at one moment it is convinced of one thing, and later it believes something quite different. At one moment it remembers something, and later it has no recollection.

No human being is inwardly stable or coherent. You should recognize honestly your instability, and cast yourself on the one who never changes.

Augustine of Hippo: Commentary on Psalm 121

The purpose of miracles

When people truly open their minds, and contemplate the way in which the universe is ordered and governed, they are amazed – they are overwhelmed by a sense of the miraculous. When people contemplate with open minds the germination of a single seed, they are equally overwhelmed. They acknowledge God's wonderful power in all things. Yet in fact most of humanity is so preoccupied with its petty concerns that it has lost the power to contemplate the works of God.

That is why God performs certain extraordinary and unexpected actions, which are called miracles. By means of these miracles God startles people, jolting them out of their spiritual lethargy. A dead man rises back to life, and people marvel; yet numerous babies are born every day, and no one marvels. If only people opened their minds, they would see that the birth of a baby, in which a new life is created, is a greater miracle than restoring life.

People hold cheap what they see every day. But when they are confronted by some unusual event, they are dumbfounded – even though that event is no more wonderful than everything else they see. The harvest that is reaped year by year is surely a greater miracle than the feeding of five thousand people with five loaves of bread; in the harvest food for an entire year is created out of few grains sown in the ground. Yet no one marvels at the harvest, because it is ordinary.

The purpose of miracles is to teach us to see the miraculous everywhere.

Augustine of Hippo: Commentary on the Gospel of John

Delight in truth and righteousness

When people take delight in truth and in righteousness, they are in fact taking delight in Christ, for Christ is truth and righteousness. And this delight is the essence of faith.

People in love would understand what I mean. People who are hungry would know what I mean. People in the desert, panting with thirst, would know what I mean. They are people who want something desperately, and would take intense delight in having what they want. The true Christian is someone who wants Christ desperately, and who takes intense delight in having Christ – in having truth and righteousness. But people with no feeling would not understand what I mean.

Offer a handful of grass to a sheep, and the sheep is drawn to you. Offer bag of nuts to a child, and the child is drawn to you. When people are offered truth and righteousness, and when they understand what is being offered, they are naturally attracted – and thus they are drawn to Christ. For what does the mind desire more strongly than truth? And what does the heart desire more strongly than righteousness?

Augustine of Hippo: Commentary on the Gospel of John

Stretching the soul

If you are a devout disciple of Christ, your desire to see God grows ever stronger; and this desire will cause its own satisfaction. Imagine that you are filling a bag; you learn that the bag is too small to hold all that you want – so you stretch the bag to make it bigger. In the same way, you soon learn as a Christian that the soul is far too small to perceive the fullness of God; but your desire for God gradually stretches your soul, so that you are able to perceive more and more of God.

But before you can stretch and fill that bag, you must first empty it of all that you do not want; if the bag contains vinegar, and you want to fill it with honey, you must first pour out the vinegar, and clean the bag thoroughly. Similarly, if you wish to see God, you must rid yourself of all worldly desires. Like cleaning a bag, this is hard work, and requires great effort.

What does the word 'God' mean? What is it that you wish to see? There is no answer, because no words can describe or define God. The word 'God' is the distillation of all human hopes. Any attempt to explain or qualify that word lessens its meaning. So stretch your soul constantly, by every means at your disposal, begging God to fill you.

Augustine of Hippo: Commentary on the Letters of John

Loving God, neighbours and self

If you love your neighbours, then you learn to love the source of love, which is God. And, since the source of love dwells within your soul, you come to know him better than you know your neighbours.

Pride prevents you from loving your neighbours, and so prevents you from knowing the source of love. Thus you must allow God to heal you of all pride, so you can serve your neighbours without restraint.

Thus the two great commandments, to love God and to love your neighbours, cannot exist without one another. By loving your neighbours, you come to know God; and by loving God, and allowing him to heal you of pride, you become generous towards your neighbours. Conversely, if you refuse to love your neighbours, whom you can see, it is impossible for you to love God, whom you cannot see.

So stop worrying how much love you should give to your neighbours, and how much you should give to God. Give to God immeasurably more love than you give to yourself; and love your neighbours as much as you love yourself. When you do this, you will discover something strange: that through loving God, you truly love yourself; and through truly loving yourself, you truly love your neighbours also.

Augustine of Hippo: On the Trinity 8

The business of prayer

If you wish to be blessed by God, you must pray to him. You do not need to use many words; you do not need to demonstrate your eloquence to him. But why, you may ask, do we need to pray at all, since God already knows our needs? God wants you to pray in order that, through the process of prayer, your desire for him may deepen – and you may thereby be more able to receive his gifts. These gifts are very great, and the human capacity to receive them is small and meagre; prayer stretches this capacity.

At certain times you must deliberately bring your mind back to the business of prayer, and detach yourself from all other matters. You need to remind yourself, through the words you use in prayer, of the glory of God. Prayer fans the fire of devotion to God; and if you do not pray frequently, this fire dies down, and eventually goes out. By means of prayer you put yourself in the presence of God, and place your desires before him.

When your other duties are less demanding, you should take the opportunity for an extended period of prayer; in this way the fire of devotion will burn even brighter. But even when you are in the midst of activity, you should cultivate the ability to pray within the depths of your mind. In this way you will learn to pray without ceasing.

Augustine of Hippo: Letters 130

Response to troubles

The perplexities and troubles of this world have three possible purposes. First, they are a remedy for human pride. Secondly, they are a means of exercising and testing human patience; and, if the test is passed, there is a rich reward. Thirdly, they are a means of eradicating specific sins. But when a particular trouble arises, you cannot tell which purpose it is serving. So you do not know how to respond; you do not know how you should pray. Thus you simply desire to rid yourself of the trouble; you pray fervently for the trouble to go away.

Since the Lord has sent you the trouble for a purpose, he is unlikely to answer your prayer. Do not infer from this that he is neglecting you. Rather, you should take it as an opportunity for learning to trust him. You should endure the trouble with patience, knowing that in the fullness of time it will bring you great blessing. Thus, through your weakness, God makes you strong.

Indeed, if anything happens in your life contrary to your prayers, you should give thanks to God, knowing that his will is far superior to your own. Through thanking God in all circumstances, you will learn to conform your will to his.

Augustine of Hippo: Letters 130

The earthly and heavenly cities

We see two cities, the earthly city and the heavenly city. They were created by two kinds of love: the earthly city was created by self-love, which leads to contempt for God; the heavenly city was created by the love of God, which leads to contempt for self. The earthly city glories in itself; the heavenly city glories in the Lord. Citizens of the earthly city boast of their own achievements; citizens of the heavenly city ascribe every achievement to God. In the earthly city people try to gain power for themselves, so they can dominate others; in the heavenly city people regard each other as equals under the sovereign power of God.

In the heavenly city the people are free; they know God, and they freely do his will. Their life is a perpetual sabbath, which has no evening. They are at leisure, blissfully gazing upon God. They see God, and love him; they love God, and praise him.

Augustine of Hippo: The City of God, Preface

The Father and the Son

The whole body of the faithful acknowledges its belief in God the Father almighty, and in Jesus Christ, his only Son, our Lord, who was born of the Holy Spirit and the Virgin Mary. This statement of faith confounds all those who wish to distort the Christian faith. Christians believe that God is both almighty and Father.

It follows that the Son is coeternal with the Father, differing in no respect from him. The Son is God, born of God; he is almighty because his Father is almighty; he is eternal because his Father is eternal. He is not later in time, nor inferior in power, nor dissimilar in glory, nor divided in essence. This same Son was born of the Holy Spirit and the Virgin Mary.

But this birth in time has taken nothing from, and added nothing to, the Son's eternal divinity. Its effects have been entirely on human beings, who had surrendered to evil and thereby placed themselves under the power of death. Human beings could not, by their own efforts, overcome evil; they are in themselves weaker than sin and death. Victory over evil was only possible by the Son taking human nature, and making it his own. Sin could not defile him, nor death enslave him, because he had been conceived of the Holy Spirit, in the womb of a virgin, whose virginity remained unblemished throughout her pregnancy.

Leo of Rome: The Tome

Fully divine and fully human

The birth of the Son, which was uniquely marvellous and marvellously unique, should not be understood as constituting a new mode of creation, which precludes the distinctive nature of humanity. While the Holy Spirit put fruitfulness into the Virgin's womb, the body of Christ came from the Virgin's own body.

Thus, the properties of both divinity and humanity were fully preserved, and came together within a single person. Humility was balanced by majesty, weakness by strength, and mortality by eternity. To pay the debt which humanity had incurred, a nature free from sin and suffering was united with a nature capable of sin and suffering. And in order to heal our sinful natures, Jesus Christ as human was able to die, while Jesus Christ as divine is unable to die.

This true God was born in the form and nature of true humanity. This person, Jesus Christ, was fully divine and fully human. His body had the same nature and properties as human bodies have had since the creation of the world. And he took on a human body in order to restore humanity to the same relationship with God that it had at the creation of the world. In Christ there is no trace of the evil that had subsequently infected human flesh.

Leo of Rome: The Tome

Empty of power

Although Jesus Christ shared our humanity and understood our weaknesses, he was not stained by our sin. He became human without detracting from the divine; and in this way he lifted humanity towards divinity. He made the invisible visible; he made the mortal immortal. This act of condescension was prompted by compassion for humanity's plight. The Son of God emptied himself of power, in order to reassert God's power over humanity.

Evil had deceived humanity, depriving human beings of divine grace – and thence depriving them of the hope of immortality. It appeared that God, bound by his own laws of justice, had been forced to alter humanity's destiny. He had created men and women with great honour; but now, owing to their submission to evil, he was forced to sentence them to death.

The only means of redeeming the situation was for the Son of God to come down from his throne in heaven and, without losing his Father's glory, to enter the world. He could only do this through a new mode of birth, by which he made his invisible divine nature visible in human flesh. Although he had existed before all time, he now began to exist within time; although he had existed outside all physical boundaries, he now began to exist within finite space.

Leo of Rome: The Tome

Yearning for God

Lord, if you are not here, where shall I seek you? But if you are everywhere, why do I not see you here? It is said that you dwell in perfect light. But where is this perfect light, and how can I reach it? Who can lead me to that light, and take me into it, that I may see you within it? What is your form and colour, that I may recognize you? Since I have never seen you, I have no notion of your form.

Most high Lord, I am like an exile, banished from your presence. I tremble with desire to see you, and yet I am far away from you. I pant with longing for you, yet I have never glimpsed your face. You are my God, you are my Lord, yet you are hidden from me. You who made me, and you who saved me from sin; all the blessings that I now enjoy, come from you. Yet I do not know you. You created me in order that I may see you; yet I have not fulfilled the purpose of my creation.

How long, O Lord, will you forget me? How long will you hide your face from me? When will you look down on me, and hear me? When will you enlighten my eyes, and show me your face? When will you restore me to your presence? Turn towards me, Lord, and reveal yourself to me. Have pity on me in my plight.

Anselm: Proslogion I

Belief and understanding

Let it be my lot to see your light – even if I see it from a distance, and from far below. Teach me the way to you; and, when I have followed that way, welcome me into your presence. I can never find you, unless you guide me; I can never see you, unless you reveal yourself to me. I seek you, Lord, because I yearn for you; and I yearn for you, because my nature is to seek you.

I thank you, Lord, that you have made me in your image, that I may remember you, think of you and love you. But that image is worn, scarred by faults and darkened by the smoke of sin. It cannot achieve that for which it was made, unless you renew and refashion it. I do not try to penetrate the depths of your being, because my capacity for knowledge is so small. Yet I long to understand some degree of truth – the truth which my heart already believes and loves.

I do not seek to understand the truth in order that I might believe it; rather, I believe the truth in order that I might understand it. For this I also believe: that unless I believe, I cannot understand.

Anselm: Proslogion i

The existence of God

Lord, you add understanding to faith. Therefore, as far as it is profitable for me, let me understand that you exist, in the way I believe you exist; and that your nature is what I believe it to be. I believe you to be that above which nothing greater can be conceived.

The fool believes in his heart that you do not exist. Is the fool correct? After all, the fool understands my notion of you, as being that above which nothing greater can be conceived; but the fool does not believe what he understands. It is one thing to have some concept in the mind; it is quite another to understand that the concept actually exists outside the mind.

A painter, when he thinks out beforehand what he is going to paint, has the picture in his mind; but he knows that it does not yet exist, because he has not painted it. But when he has painted the picture, he knows that it exists in reality, as well as in his mind. In the same way the fool agrees that the notion of you – the notion of that above which nothing greater can be conceived – exists in his mind. But he disputes whether you exist in reality.

But something above which nothing greater can be conceived, cannot exist only in the mind. If it exists in the mind, it is possible for it to exist in reality; and if it exists in reality, it would be greater than merely existing in the mind.

Anselm: Proslogion 2

The nature of God

Since you cannot be conceived not to exist, Lord, you must exist. If you did not exist in reality, you would not be the greatest entity that can be conceived. The greatest entity that can be conceived, must exist both in the mind and in reality; if it did not exist in reality, it would not be the greatest entity that can be conceived

I declare, Lord, that you exist – because you cannot be conceived as not to exist. If any creature could conceive of a being greater than you, that creature would rise above its creator; and that would be absurd. Whatever else exists, apart from you, can be conceived as not to exist. But you alone must be conceived as existing in reality.

Thus, no one who truly understands what God is, can think that God does not exist. People may say that God does not exist, but their words have no meaning. God is the highest entity that the human mind can conceive. Those who truly understand this, also understand that he must exist; it is impossible to conceive otherwise. Those who grasp the nature of God, cannot conceive of him not existing.

What are you, Lord God, above whom nothing greater can be conceived? You exist alone above all things, and you have made everything else out of nothing. No good quality can be lacking in you, because you are the highest good. Thus you are just, true, generous – and whatever else it is better to be than not to be.

Anselm: Proslogion 4, 5

Sin and power

How can you be omnipotent, Lord, if you cannot do all things? How can you claim to do all things, if you cannot sin – if you cannot lie, and cannot falsify the truth? If you cannot sin, you cannot claim to be able to do all things. Or does the capacity for sin come not from power, but from lack of power – not from the ability to do evil, but from the inability to prevent evil? Indeed, sinners are those with so little control over themselves, that they cannot stop themselves from doing harm; they are at the mercy of forces which they are too weak to oppose.

I conclude that those who have the power to commit sin, are lacking in power. And the greater is a person's power to commit sin, the more powerless that person is. Thus, Lord God, you are in fact truly omnipotent, because you cannot act through powerlessness.

Anselm: Proslogion 7

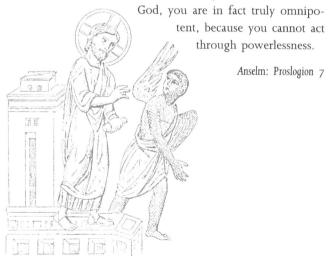

Compassion and transcendence

Lord God, how can you be both compassionate and above passion? If you are above passion, you cannot share people's suffering; but if you cannot share suffering, you cannot be compassionate — since compassion consists in feeling miserable at the misery of others. And if you are not compassionate, from where can we derive consolation during unhappy times?

The answer must be that you are compassionate in terms of our experience, and not compassionate in terms of your own being. When you look upon us in our misery, we experience the effect of compassion, but you do not experience the feeling. You demonstrate compassion when you heal the sick and pardon the sinner; but you do not feel their suffering within yourself.

Anselm: Proslogion 8

Justice and goodness

Lord God, you are supremely just; and yet, out of your supreme goodness, you are kind to sinners. You would be less good if you refused to show kindness to sinners. Those who are kind to both the righteous and the wicked, are better than those who are kind to the good alone. And those who are kind to the wicked, by both punishing them and forgiving them, are better than those whose kindness is confined to punishment alone.

The depth of your goodness, Lord, is beyond human imagination. We see the consequences of your goodness, but not its source. We see the river flowing, but we cannot see the spring from which it rises. It is from the abundance of your goodness that you are kind to those who sin against you.

Justice demands that you should reward only those who are righteous, and should merely punish those who are wicked. So when you are kind to the wicked, we gasp in amazement. Out of justice you bless the righteous; and out of kindness you bless the wicked. And when sinners acknowledge your kindness, then you forgive them – after which you can bless them out of justice.

It is hard for us to understand how your goodness does not conflict with your justice. Yet we must believe that the two are consistent, because there can be no justice without goodness.

Anselm: Proslogion 9

Infinity and eternity

Whatever you are, Lord, you are nothing other than yourself. You are the life whereby you live; you are the wisdom with which you are wise; you are the goodness whereby you are good to the righteous and the wicked alike; you are all the attributes which you express.

Anything that is bounded by space and time, is less than that which is boundless. Since nothing is greater than you, Lord, you are not bounded by space and time; you are everywhere and always; you are infinite and eternal.

Are you alone in being infinite and eternal? Any material object is either in one place or in another; it cannot be in more than one place at once. Moreover, any event either occurs at one time or at another; the same event cannot occur more than once. But this is not true of the soul. The soul is fully present in every part of the body; and the soul is unchanged from one moment to the next. You, Lord, are infinite and eternal by your own nature; and through your infinity and eternity the soul is also infinite and eternal.

Anselm: Proslogion 13

Self-knowledge

There are two things you need to know: first, what you are; and secondly, who made you what you are. If you know both these things, you will boast – but not in yourself and in your own power. If you do not know who you are, let your friends teach you. If you do not know who made you what you are, this ignorance puts you on the same level as an animal.

Some people ignore the gift of reason within them and behave like animals. They turn away from the glory inside themselves, and are slaves to their own senses. They are carried away by their own desires, and thus they become no better than animals. We should be terrified by this kind of ignorance, which makes people undervalue themselves.

But we should be equally terrified of the ignorance that makes people think too highly of themselves. This happens when people think that they are the source of good within themselves. But there is something even more detestable than ignorance. This is the pride by which people, in full knowledge of the truth, dare to boast of their own goodness. Even though they know they are not the source of goodness within themselves, they pretend that they are. Thus, they are stealing the glory that belongs to God.

The first kind of ignorance has no glory. The second has glory, but not in God's sight; knowledge combined with pride is an act of treason against God.

Bernard of Clairvaux: On Loving God 2

The purpose of suffering

To love your neighbours with perfect justice, it is necessary to be prompted by God. How can you love your neighbours perfectly, if your love is not inspired by God? But if you do not love God, how can you be inspired by him?

This is how God causes you to love him. God not only created all creatures, he also protects them. Indeed, he created all creatures in such a way that they depend on his protection. To ensure that human beings recognize God's protection – and hence to prevent them from imagining that they do not need him – God decided that human beings should endure suffering. When they suffer, human beings naturally turn to God for help; and thus they honour God as he deserves.

Human beings are bodily creatures; so, left to themselves, they do not know how to love anything except themselves. But through suffering they begin to love God – not for God's sake, but for their own benefit. Gradually they learn that God is the source of all that is good, and that without God they are helpless.

Bernard of Clairvaux: On Loving God 8

The presence of God's Word

The Word of God has come to me many times, penetrating my soul. Yet I have never been aware of the moment of his coming. I perceive his presence, and I remember afterwards that he has been with me. Sometimes I even have an inkling that he will come. But I am never conscious of his coming and going. And where he comes from, where he goes after leaving, and by what means he enters and withdraws, I cannot say.

The coming of the Word is not visible to my eyes, since he has no colour. He is not audible to my ears, since he makes no sound. I do not sense him in my nostrils, since he has no fragrance. I cannot taste him, because he cannot be eaten. And I cannot touch him, because he is not tangible.

How then does he enter? Perhaps he does not enter, because he does not come from outside. Indeed, he does not exist outside us, like a material object. Yet nor does he come from inside me; he is perfectly good, whereas I have no good within me. Even if I reach up to the highest spiritual level of which I am capable, he is still towering above me. In my curiosity I have descended to the deepest level of understanding of which I am capable, and he is still below me.

If I look outside myself, he is stretching far beyond the horizon. If I look within myself, he is further inside me than I can see. Yes, in him I live, and move, and exist.

Bernard of Clairvaux: On the Song of Songs 74

The self-sufficiency of love

Love is self-sufficient; it is pleasing to itself, and on its own account. Love is its own payment, its own reward. Love needs no cause and no result; love is its own result. Love has intrinsic value, and is not desired as a means to something else. I love because I love; I love in order to love.

Love constantly returns to God, who is its divine source. It must always draw from that infinite source, that spring which never runs dry. God loves all his creatures and he wishes only to be loved in return; indeed, he loves for no other purpose than to evoke love. He knows that all who love him, find happiness in their love.

Bernard of Clairvaux: On the Song of Songs 83

Threefold coming of the Lord

We have come to know a threefold coming of the Lord. The third coming takes place between the other two; they are clearly manifest, but the third is not. In the first coming the Lord was seen on earth, and lived among men and women; people saw him in human form. In the last coming every human being shall see him in regal splendour, and realize that in him alone they can be saved. The other coming is hidden. This occurs when people recognize him within themselves, and are overwhelmed by him. In brief, the first coming was in flesh and in weakness; the intermediate coming is in spirit and in power; the last coming will be in glory and majesty.

This intermediate coming is like a road leading from the first to the last coming. In the first coming Christ was our redemption; in the last he will appear as our salvation; in the intermediate coming he is our rest and comfort.

If you desire this intermediate coming, obey Christ's commands. Let his teachings pierce your soul, penetrating all your emotions and actions. Take delight in his sayings. If you keep Christ's commands close to your heart, you will be kept by him. He will come to you, cherish you and renew you. Outwardly you will still be an earthly being; but inwardly you will become a heavenly being.

Bernard of Clairvaux: On Advent 5

Kindness made flesh

Before God appeared in human form, his kindness lay partly hidden. Of course, God was always kind; his kindness existed from all eternity. But how could human beings know its greatness? It was a promise, made through prophets, that had not yet been fully experienced; so many did not believe in it.

Now his kindness is no longer a promise, but has been conferred. It is no longer delayed, but has been given. It is no longer predicted, but has been bestowed. It is as if God has sent down from heaven to earth a bag filled with mercy – a bag that in our desperation we tear open, pouring out the contents. It is a small bag, but it is full; Jesus Christ came as a tiny baby, but the fullness of God was present within him.

The fullness of God came at the fullness of time. He came in the flesh, that he might make himself manifest to our human minds; and in this way we can know the full extent of his kindness. When God became human, his kindness could no longer be concealed.

When you look upon Christ, rejoice in the knowledge that God cares for you personally. When you look upon the sufferings of Christ, rejoice in the knowledge that God shares your sufferings, and is filled with compassion. When you look upon God in human flesh, rejoice in the knowledge that he can make you divine.

Bernard of Clairvaux: On Epiphany 1

The first proof of God's existence

God's existence can be proven in five ways. The first and most obvious proof concerns change.

It is manifest that things in this world are in a continuous process of change. And anything undergoing change is being changed by something else. An entity in the process of change cannot yet be perfect; but the fact of its changing implies that it is capable of improvement, and hence eventually capable of perfection. But the entity causing change must already be perfect – because only by being perfect in itself could it cause other entities to become perfect. By analogy we may observe fire and wood: fire is already hot, and wood is capable of becoming hot; it follows that fire can make wood hot.

There may, of course, be intermediate causes of change, which are not already perfect – and hence themselves are capable of being changed. But the ultimate cause of change must itself be unchangeable, and hence perfect. This ultimate cause is what we understand by God.

Thomas Aquinas: Summa of Theology I

The second proof of God's existence

The second proof of God's existence concerns the nature of causation.

In the world we observe causes in an order of succession. We never see, nor could we see, any entity causing itself – for that would imply it existed before its own existence, which is absurd. Any succession of causes must begin somewhere.

There may be a countless number of intermediate causes; but these intermediate causes are links in a chain of causation starting with a first cause, which has not itself been caused. Each intermediate cause is in itself an effect of an earlier link in the chain; but there must be a first cause that is not also an effect. Without this first cause none of the intermediate causes could function, and so there would be no effects. Yet this contradicts our observation; we see effects all around us all the time.

This first cause in the chain of cause and effect is what we understand by God.

Thomas Aquinas: Summa of Theology I

The third proof of God's existence

The third proof of God's existence concerns the existence of the unnecessary and the necessary.

Our experience includes entities capable of existing, but apparently unnecessary, since they come and go. If an entity is unnecessary, it must once not have existed. But every entity cannot be unnecessary, for this would imply that at some point in the past nothing existed. And if at some point nothing existed, then nothing could exist now – since all unnecessary entities must be brought into existence by something else.

It follows that not every entity can be unnecessary; there must be at least one entity that necessarily exists. An entity that necessarily exists, may or may not have derived this necessity from something else. But, as with the succession of causes, there must be a necessary entity whose necessity does not derive from any other entity.

This necessary entity is what we understand by God.

Thomas Aquinas: Summa of Theology I

The fourth proof of God's existence

The fourth proof of God's existence concerns the gradation of things.

There are some living entities that are better, truer, nobler and so on; and there are other entities that are less good, less true, less noble and so on. But such comparisons imply the existence of the superlative – the entity that is best, truest, noblest and so on. Moreover, the entity which is best, must make other living entities good; the entity which is truest, must confer degrees of truth on other living entities; the entity which is noblest, must confer degrees of nobility on other living entities; and so on.

Heat may be used as an analogy. We may say that one thing is hotter than another thing; but this comparison is in relation to that which is hottest, namely fire. Moreover, it is fire that makes other entities hot.

It follows that there must be a being that has every moral and spiritual quality at the highest level, and which confers these qualities on other entities. This superlative entity is what we understand by God.

Thomas Aquinas: Summa of Theology I

The fifth proof of God's existence

The fifth proof of God's existence concerns order.

When we observe nature, we discern its tendency towards order rather than chaos. When living entities follow the laws of their own nature, even when they are not aware of those laws, their actions are directed towards certain goals; and usually their actions achieve those goals.

These goals, which dwell within all living entities, cannot exist by accident; if they existed by accident, we should discern chaos all around us, rather than order. On the contrary, the goals must have been implanted by an entity that is fully aware of the meaning and importance of each goal – and of how the achievement of one goal by one living entity relates to the achievement of goals by all other living entities. Order would only exist in nature if a single omniscient entity implanted all goals within all living entities.

This single omniscient entity is what we understand by God.

Thomas Aquinas: Summa of Theology 1

Maintaining existence

All living entities are maintained in existence by God.

There are two ways for one entity to preserve another. The first is indirect, when a potential cause of destruction is removed. For example, if a father prevents his child from falling into a fire, he is said to have preserved the child. God from time to time preserves entities in this fashion; but for much of the time entities do not require this kind of intervention.

The second is direct, when one entity so depends on another entity, that it cannot exist even for a moment without it. It is in this direct sense that all living entities are preserved by God. All entities so depend on God, that none could exist for a single moment without him.

We may see this distinction by comparison with warmth and light. Hot water in a pan remains hot, even after the pan has been removed from the fire; but from time to time the pan must be put on the fire, to prevent the water becoming cold. Space, however, cannot remain light even for a moment after the source of light has been removed. The relationship of all living entities to God is akin to that of space to light.

Thomas Aquinas: Summa of Theology I

Intellect, will and belief

When we are faced with a contradiction, in which there are two opposing views, the intellect can respond in different ways. Sometimes it does not incline one way or another, whether because of lack of evidence, or because of the equality of evidence on both sides. Thus, the intellect wavers between two views, and is in a state of doubt. Sometimes the intellect is inclined more to one side than the other; yet the evidence is not of sufficient weight to demand complete assent. Thus the intellect is in a state of opinion.

Sometimes the intellect is immediately convinced that one view is right, because it conforms to fundamental axioms. Thus, the intellect is in a state of knowledge. Sometimes the intellect does not incline one way or the other, because neither view is manifestly in conformity with fundamental axioms. But the will chooses to assent to one view, definitely and positively, through some influence that can move the will, but not the intellect. This influence is such that the will regards it as good and right to assent to one view.

This is the state of belief. We believe in the words of a particular person, because to believe seems proper and advantageous. In particular we are moved to believe in certain sayings when it seems that eternal life depends on belief.

Thomas Aquinas: On Truth 14

Inward and outward work

Inward work – work within the soul – is godly, because it is aimed at making the soul more god-like. Outward work, regardless of its quality and magnitude, its length and breadth, does not in any way increase the value of inward work. Even in a thousand lifetimes outward work could not make a person more similar to God.

Inward work is good in all manner of ways. If our inward work is feeble and worthless, our outward work will be feeble and worthless too. If our inward work is great, it will make our outward work great as well. If our inward work draws its goodness from the heart of God, and from nowhere else, it receives the Son into the soul; and the soul is thereby reborn as a son in the bosom of the heavenly Father.

Outward work does not draw goodness directly from God, but receives its goodness from inward work. Outward work is complex, and its value is measured by its quality; in these respects it is foreign and alien to God. Outward work clings and adheres to inward work, and thus finds serenity and light; but in itself it is blind, without direction or purpose.

Eckhart: Book of Divine Consolation 2

The birth of God in the soul

Through inward work God's Son is born in the soul and the soul is born as a child of God. The Son of God in the soul is the spring and source of the Holy Spirit; thus, as the Spirit enters the soul, it brings to birth God's Son within the soul. God's Son is the origin of all who are children of God. Only through the birth of God's Son in the soul can a person be restored to God's image.

Those in whom God's Son has been born, are estranged from all quantity and complexity, including even the complexity of the orders of angels. Indeed, they are estranged from goodness, truth and all things that allow any shades of difference or distinction. They are entrusted to God, who cannot be conceived, and who has no complexity – in whom the Father, the Son and the Holy Spirit are stripped of all differences and attributes, and totally unified. This unity blesses us.

The further away we are from the unity of God, the less we are children of God, and hence the less perfectly the Holy Spirit springs up in us and flows from us. The nearer we are to the unity of God, the more fully we are children of God, and the more perfectly the Holy Spirit flows from us.

Eckhart: *Book of Divine Consolation* 2

The mind fixed on God

If God is in you, then he remains in you wherever you go. When you walk down the street, or visit friends, he is with you – just as much as when you are in church, in the desert, or in a monastic cell. No one and nothing can obstruct you.

Why is this so? Because the mind is totally fixed on God. Your only intention is to serve God. For you all objects and all events are divine. You carry God with you wherever you go, and in whatever action you perform. Indeed, all your actions are performed by God; this is because he is the cause of your actions, and is responsible for them. By concentrating your mind purely and simply on God, you ensure that he is working in and through you; so neither your circumstances, nor the people around you, can hinder you. You aim for nothing and seek nothing, except to unite your endeavours with God's; and you want no reward except the knowledge that you are doing his will.

Just as God cannot be disturbed by complexity and difficulty, in the same way nothing will upset or disturb your thoughts. In God all complexity is simplicity, and all difficulty is blessing.

Eckhart: Talks of Instruction 6

God in all people

You should train yourself to keep God always present in your mind, in your actions and in your will. Watch over yourself to ensure that God is present – whether you are outside in the clamour of the world, or inside a church.

This does not mean that all places and all activities are equally valuable. On the contrary, it is better to pray than to spin; and it is better to be in a church than in a public square. But you should retain the inner attitude – the same trust and love for God, and the same seriousness of intent. If your attitude of mind is constantly godly, then nothing can disturb your inner serenity.

So how can you develop this serenity; how can you ensure that God is always present within you? Look for God deep within your soul. There you will find a sublime movement towards God; you will observe the soul constantly striving to know him. Do not attempt constantly to think about God; that is impossible, since any train of thought always comes to an end. Rather, you should become aware of the soul's innate activity and you should live in accordance with it.

The soul is the image of God within you. Thus, by becoming aware of your own soul, you will see the image of God in all other men and women – and you will naturally behave towards them in a godly manner.

Eckhart: Talks of Instruction 6

Activities in the world

There are different kinds of work; but whatever is done in the right spirit is of equal value. If you possess God, if you are aware of divine activity within your soul, then God will shine in all you do. His light will radiate from you in secular activities, just as much as in religious ones. Of course, this does not mean you can deliberately engage in corrupt and evil pursuits. Rather, you will want to offer to God all you do, all you see and all you hear. Thus your intellect will be directed entirely to doing God's will.

Some people think that the only way to avoid evil, is to withdraw from the world, and do nothing. But in truth the mere fact of being human compels all of us to engage in some activity. So you should not be afraid of working in the world. Before starting any activity, you should spend some time enlisting God's help through prayer, fixing your heart and mind firmly upon him, and striving to unite your intentions with his.

Avoid complacency. When you have completed some activity, do not congratulate yourself on how well you have done. On the contrary, look critically at yourself, asking how you could have done better. This will ensure that you never become casual or lazy.

Eckhart: Talks of Instruction 7, 8

Flesh and soul

I lay down these two propositions concerning liberty and servitude: the Christian is utterly free, subject to no one; and the Christian is the most dutiful servant, subject to everyone.

Human beings have a twofold nature, spiritual and bodily. The spiritual nature, which is called the soul, is made new through Christ; the bodily nature, which is called the flesh, remains old. Thus these two natures are opposed to one another.

Since the bodily nature cannot be made new, there is nothing to be gained from dressing in religious robes, living in religious places, undertaking religious activities, fasting for religious purposes and so on. All these things relate to the body, and hence are wasted; besides, they encourage hypocrisy, since they can be done without any devotion to God.

In order to justify the soul before God, and hence set the soul free, a quite different approach is required. The soul cannot be harmed by profane clothes, by living in profane places and by eating and drinking in the normal fashion. More importantly, no exertion by the soul, such as theological speculation or meditation, can help the soul. One thing, and one thing alone, can justify and liberate the soul: faith in the holy Word of God.

Martin Luther: Concerning Christian Liberty

Faith and works

The soul can do without everything except the Word of God. Without the Word of God, none of its wants are met; but with the Word of God, it is abundantly rich, and wants for nothing. The soul needs God's Word for life and liberty; it needs God's Word in order to be justified before God. Thus we say that the soul is justified by faith alone – by faith in God's Word – and not by any good works.

We note that God gives commands and makes promises. His commands tell us what we should do but they do not give us the power to do it. His promises are words of truth, liberty and peace which feed the soul; the soul puts faith in these promises, and hence becomes attached to them, and even absorbed by them.

Thus we see why faith has such power, and why no good works can compare with it. Iron, when it is exposed to fire, glows like fire. In the same way the soul, when it is exposed by faith to God's Word, becomes divine.

This does not mean that we should ignore God's commands, and become careless or wicked. Rather it means that faith gives us the power to obey God's commands.

Martin Luther: Concerning Christian Liberty

The priesthood of all believers

Through faith we honour the object of faith. By putting their complete trust in God's Word, faithful Christians demonstrate their reverence for God.

Through faith the soul is united with Christ, as a wife is united with her husband. Christ and the soul become a single entity.

When we reflect upon the nature of faith, we recognize its supreme value. Without faith the soul is full of sin; and it is destined to be condemned to death. But with faith the soul is full of grace; it has been forgiven, and has been granted eternal life. Through putting our faith in God's word, God takes away sin, suffering and death; and in their place he puts righteousness, joy and life. A good husband takes away from his wife all that is bad, and replaces it with all that is good; God is the perfect husband to the soul.

Through faith we become as free as kings. Also we become priests. Priesthood is a far higher dignity than kingship. As priests we are worthy to converse with God, to pray to God for others, and to teach one another about God. Every Christian believer is worthy to be a priest.

Martin Luther: *Concerning Christian Liberty*

Good works

We do not reject good works; on the contrary, we embrace them with passion. We do not condemn good works; we condemn the idea that good works can bring salvation.

As a faithful Christian you do not live for yourself alone, working only on your own behalf. You live for all people on earth. You make your body the servant of your soul, in order that you may serve others sincerely and freely. You take care of your body, in order that, through its health and fitness, you may help those in need. To the extent that you are strong, you willingly carry the burdens of the weak. You regard every person as you regard yourself – as a child of God.

From your faith flows love, and from your love flows joy, and from your joy flows an eagerness to help your neighbours, without taking into account gratitude or ingratitude, praise or blame, gain or loss. In helping your neighbours you have no intention of putting them under an obligation to help you. You do not distinguish between friendly neighbours and hostile ones, but treat all with the same kindness. In this way you imitate God, who distributes his material gifts to all people, the just and the unjust alike.

Martin Luther: *Concerning Christian Liberty*

True faith

Faith is not that human idea and notion which some people call faith. People hear and speak a great deal about faith. When they see someone whose life is not improving, and who performs only a few good works, they are apt to say quite erroneously: 'Faith is not enough; a person must do good works in order to be justified and saved.' They make this error because, when they hear the gospel, they work hard to generate within themselves a mental state in which they can say: 'I believe.' And they take this to be true faith. But this kind of faith is a human attitude, which can never reach the depths of the heart; so nothing comes of it, and it leads to no improvement of life.

True faith is a work of God within us. It is the means by which God causes us to be born anew. It kills the old self, and transforms us in heart, soul, mind and faculties; and it brings with it the Holy Spirit.

This faith is a living, busy, active and powerful thing; a person with faith finds it impossible to refrain from doing good works. It does not ask whether there are good works to be done; before the question arises, it has already done them. Faith is a vibrant and courageous confidence in God's grace. It is so deep and solid, that believers would stake their lives on it a thousand times. This confidence makes people joyful, bold and happy in their relationship with God and with other people.

Martin Luther: Preface to the Letter to the Romans

A personal creed

This is my personal creed.

I believe that God has created me, and has given me for my benefit a body, with its various organs and limbs, and a soul; that he daily bestows on me clothes and shoes, food and drink, house and furnishings, wife and children, fields and cattle, and all other necessites and comforts; and that he protects me from both physical and spiritual danger. I believe that he does this out of pure and fatherly goodness, and not in response to any merit on my part; and thus I am bound to thank and praise him, and also serve and obey him.

I believe that Jesus Christ has redeemed me. I believe that I was lost in sin, and condemned to eternal punishment; and that Jesus Christ has delivered me from all sin and punishment, not with gold and silver, but with his holy and precious blood, shed during his suffering and death. I believe that through this redemption I now belong to Christ, and live under his rule, serving him as he demands; and that I shall rise with him to eternal life.

I believe that I am incapable, through my own efforts and understanding, of attaining faith in Jesus Christ; but that the Holy Spirit has called me to faith, illuminated me with spiritual insight, and made me holy.

Martin Luther: *The Short Catechism*

The Word and the Spirit

By a mutual bond the Lord has joined together his Word and his Spirit. In this way, when the Spirit shines, the perfect religion of the Word may dwell in your minds. The Spirit enables you to contemplate the face of God. You, for your part, are able to embrace the Spirit with no fear of being deceived, because the Word enables you to recognize the Spirit – the Word and the Spirit being reflections of one another. God did not reveal his Word to the world for some momentary display, with the intention of withdrawing his Word when the Spirit came. Rather he sent down his Spirit by the same power with which he revealed his Word, in order to complete the work of the Word.

Faith in the Word of God does not occur if you merely think about the Word with your minds. The Word must take root in your hearts. Thus, it becomes an invisible weapon against temptation. Without the Word the heart's distrust of God is far greater than the mind's blindness; hence it is far harder for the heart to learn to trust God, than for the mind to understand God. When the Spirit comes, the mind is enlightened by the truth; and then the power of the truth must take hold of the heart. So the Spirit serves as a seal, confirming within the heart those divine promises that the mind has already accepted.

John Calvin: The Institutes I

Unity with Christ

Christ has made himself known to you, blessing you with numerous gifts, and making you a member of himself, so that you can live in unity with him. Thus, his righteousness overwhelms your sins, and his salvation wipes out your condemnation; in his worthiness he intercedes, that your unworthiness may not be brought to God's attention.

You can never separate Christ from yourself, or yourself from Christ. Christ is not outside you, but within you. Not only has he tied you to himself with an unbreakable bond of love but in his wonderful grace he has entered you. And as he enters you more fully, you will become wholly united with him.

John Calvin:
The Institutes I

Justified and sanctified

It is said that faith has justified you before God. Why? Because by faith you grasp Christ's righteousness, through which you are reconciled to God. Yet you could not grasp this righteousness without at the same time being sanctified and made holy. Christ justifies no one that he does not also sanctify.

These benefits are joined together by a permanent and indissoluble bond, so that those whom he illumines with his wisdom, he also redeems; those whom he redeems, he justifies; and those whom he justifies, he sanctifies and makes holy

Do you wish to attain righteousness in Christ? You must first possess Christ. Yet you cannot possess Christ without first sharing his holiness, because Christ cannot be divided into pieces. Christ sacrificed himself that you might be both justified and sanctified; he bestows both blessings at the same time, never giving one without the other. You are justified and made righteous by faith; and by the same process you are sanctified and made holy. And when you are holy, you overflow with good works.

John Calvin: The Institutes 3

Becoming holy

Sanctification consists in directing your emotions and desires wholly towards God. But progress is slow. Your emotions are naturally selfish and your desires physical, and you lack the strength to redirect them. Your own body seems to weigh you down; you limp, and even crawl along the ground. Yet at the moment you acquire faith the process begins, and little by little your emotions and desires are transformed.

Do not cease your efforts. Do not despair at the slowness of your progress. Even though you yearn to become holy at once, every step is worthwhile. All that matters is that you are further forward today than yesterday. Watch over yourself, to ensure that you remain sincere in your desire to reach your goal – which is to be like Christ. Never congratulate yourself on your spiritual achievements and be honest in admitting your errors and sins.

The process of becoming holy will last the entire span of your life; it is only complete when you cast off your body, and enter total union with God.

John Calvin: The Institutes 3

The faculty of choice

Human beings possess the faculty of choice. This is the ability of the mind to make judgements about things proposed to it and the ability to transmit these choices to the will, so they are enacted. To understand the faculty of choice more fully, we must look at the three stages in the moral development of humanity.

The first stage is that of childish innocence. The mind has a clear perception of God's truth and glory, and loves what it perceives.

The second stage is that of perversity. The mind becomes aware of evil, and the heart finds it beautiful and attractive. The mind is tempted to believe that the pursuit of evil is the only hope of happiness.

The third stage is that of insight. The mind discerns the difference between good and evil, and understands how the two are incompatible. Thus, true and mature choice is now possible.

Jesus Christ helps us to choose good and reject evil. He shows us the beauty of goodness; and he kindles within the heart the desire for goodness. But this does not occur instantly; it takes place gradually, and depends on constant reflection on his life and teachings.

Jacob Arminius: Disputation 11

Christian liberty

Liberty in the general sense is the state in which people are free to act as they wish, and are not bound to act in particular ways. The opposite of liberty is bondage or slavery, in which they are subject to the commands and prohibitions of others. Christian liberty is the liberty that Christ procured.

This liberty belongs to those who believe in Christ. In order to become true believers, people must first recognize their servitude: that they are in bondage to sin, and hence to death. There are four stages by which human beings are freed from this bondage.

The first is freedom from the guilt of sin, and the punishment which it deserves. This is purchased by the blood of Christ on the cross.

The second is deliverance from the tyranny of sin within the mind and the heart. This is attained by the mind and the heart freely choosing to be open to the power of the Holy Spirit.

The third is obedience to the moral laws of God. Although he could demand obedience, God simply invites us to obey his laws, leaving us free to accept or reject that invitation.

The fourth is freedom from the external rules of worship, through having direct access to God in prayer. The individual who trusts God in Christ, can speak and listen to God, without the mediation of priests and their ceremonies.

Jacob Arminius: Disputation 20

Divine providence

The nature of God, the nature of the creation, the testimony of the scriptures, and the testimony of human experience, all indicate the benign providence of God.

Providence is not an intrinsic quality of God nor is it some kind of divine habit. God does not need to express providential care for his creation, in order to be God. Providence is an expression of divine choice. Providence may be defined as God's continual care for the world, and for every creature that lives in the world. God watches over every creature's feelings and actions. And especially he watches over men and women who have put their trust in him. God in his providence works for the good of all creatures.

The good of a creature is defined by the nature of the creature, and by the relationship of the creature and God. Divine providence is the process by which God ensures good relations with all creatures, in order that their natures may be fulfilled. The actions of God in his providence demonstrate his wisdom. In his wisdom he is sometimes severe and sometimes merciful; but always he is just.

Jacob Arminius: Disputation 28

The operation of providence

We may distinguish two aspects of divine providence. The first is preservation, by which God sustains all creatures. The second is government, by which God guides their feelings and actions.

We may also distinguish four ways in which providence operates. The first is motion, by which God prompts creatures to feel and act in a particular fashion.

The second is assistance, by which God strengthens the good inclinations of creatures. The third is concurrence, by which God supports and opposes the feelings and actions of creatures. And the fourth is permission, by which God allows his creatures to feel and act in a particular fashion.

Jacob Arminius: Disputation 28

The parts and the whole

Contemplate the whole of nature in its dazzling beauty and complexity. Contemplate the universe in its awesome vastness, with the earth as a mere speck within it. Then realize that your rational mind cannot comprehend the complexity of nature or the vastness of the universe. Yet where reason must stop, imagination can proceed.

The imagination can rejoice in its own simplicity, as compared with nature's complexity; and it can thus find peace by resting in nature's ample bosom. The imagination can rejoice in its own smallness, recognizing that within the infinity of space everywhere is the centre.

If we look honestly at ourselves, we recognize the severe limitations of our knowledge. We cannot possibly comprehend the whole of God's creation. Yet we aspire to comprehend those parts to which our mental capacity bears some proportion. Then we begin to realize that every part of God's creation is connected and linked together; so that by understanding what we can, we have an inkling of the whole.

Blaise Pascal: Thoughts 72

Disagreements pointing to truth

Let us see how people define the greatest, and find out the extent to which their definitions agree. Some say the greatest good consists in virtue; others say it consists in obedience to the laws of nature; others in truth; others in the admission of ignorance; others in indolence and self-indulgence; others in abstinence from superficial pleasures; others in serenity and in never being surprised; others in doubt and scepticism.

And there are some very wise people who say that the greatest good can never be defined, however strongly we want to define it. That is the finest answer – the agreement to which our disagreements point.

Blaise Pascal: Thoughts 73

Bad and good religion

The way of God, who is gentle in all things, is to instil religion into our minds through reasoned arguments, and into our hearts with grace. But if we attempt to instil religion into people's minds by force, with threats of retribution, we instil only terror. Indeed, much of what passes for religion, is terror.

Many people hate religion. And hatred is deepened because they are afraid it might be true. The cure for this is first to show that religion is not contrary to reason, and should thus be taken seriously. Secondly, make religion attractive, so that good people want it to be true. Thirdly, explain to them that religion can help them to understand themselves and, in this way, bring them many blessings.

Blaise Pascal: Thoughts 185, 187

The gamble and the way of faith

One should be much more afraid of rejecting religious faith, and later finding out it were true, than of embracing religious faith, and later finding out it were false.

There are three ways of having faith: reason, habit and inspiration. Christianity will not accept people as true children unless they have inspiration. This does not mean that Christianity excludes reason and habit. Indeed, it requires that we open our minds to the rational foundations of its teachings, and allow our habits of thought and behaviour to be changed. But this change can only be achieved if God inspires it.

Faith tells us what the senses cannot; but true faith does not contradict the senses. Faith is above, not against, the senses.

If we make reason the only judge of truth, our religion will become devoid of mystery. But if we ignore reason, our religion will become absurd and ridiculous.

Blaise Pascal: Thoughts 241, 245, 265, 273

The beginning of religion

From time to time every person is overwhelmed by a feeling of unity: an intermingling of the self with all the objects of the senses. These moments come and go, they fade and return; indeed, they can pass so swiftly that they seem scarcely to have occurred in the realm of time. I only wish they would last long enough to inform and guide all our activities, from the mundane to the most elevated. I cannot directly describe these moments, so I must use metaphors.

They are like dew on blossoms and berries; they are like the modest and tender kiss of a maiden; they are sacred and fruitful like a bride's embrace. They are the initial encounters of the individual with the universal – although they fill no span of time, and have no tangible consequences. They are the marriage of divine and human reason; they transcend all errors and mistakes; they consummate all creative passions.

When they happen, you lie, as it were, in the bosom of infinity. You feel as if infinite power and eternal life are your own possessions. Your body, its every organ and muscle, is penetrated by divine energy. These moments are points of beginning, when life itself is reborn. These moments truly belong to you, and from them religion arises.

Friedrich Schleiermacher: On Religion

Universal miracles

What is a miracle? For religious people it is a sign or inti-
mation. Thus, to speak of an event as a miracle is to describe
the observer as well as the event itself. A miracle is an event
that both draws attention to itself, and points beyond itself.
Yet in this respect every event is miraculous, because everything that occurs in this finite realm, points towards the infinite realm; all that is finite, is part of the infinite whole.

Does the fact that we refer to some events as miracles,
while other events are not given this description, imply that
some events have a more direct relationship with the infinite?
No; 'miracle' is simply the religious term for an event. Every
event, even the most mundane, is seen as a miracle once the
religious perspective becomes predominant. For many people
only strange and inexplicable events are miraculous. But for
me all events are miracles. And the more religious you become, the more miraculous the world around you appears.

Friedrich Schleiermacher: On Religion

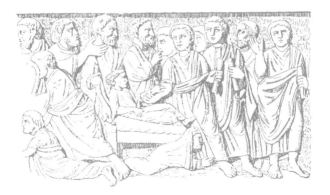

Revelation and prophecy

How does God reveal himself to us? Every new and original communication to human beings about the universe and its meaning is a divine revelation. Thus, every moment is potentially revelatory, if you are properly conscious of its inner character. And every consequence of every moment adds to the revelation. We cannot logically demonstrate that this is the case, because it lies beyond conscious observation. Yet we must not simply speak about revelation in general terms.

Individuals must judge for themselves whether an event is merely normal, without any revelatory character, or whether it is new and original. Have you never experienced the sense of newness and originality in an event? If not, then I urge you to make yourself open to the possibility that events are not mere repetitions of similar events in the past, but are fresh disclosures of the meaning of the universe.

Revelation is enhanced by prophecy. And prophecy is not concerned with accurate predictions of the future; it is concerned with how we should react to future events – and hence how our reactions shape future events. Individuals may be said to have a prophetic gift if they are able to grasp the religious dimension of events – if they are able to see the miraculous and revelatory character of events.

Friedrich Schleiermacher: On Religion

Inspiration and grace

When we speak of inspiration, what do we mean? Inspiration is simply the religious term for a sense of true morality – which is also a sense of true freedom. By morality I do not mean merely those occasions when we make deliberate choices about right and wrong. No; by true morality I mean the connection between the inner heart and outward action. If this connection is made, individuals act justly, regardless of external pressures and influences. And this connection engenders freedom, because it frees individuals from slavery to worldly demands and attachments.

Religious people often speak about the operation of grace. By grace we mean nothing other than a general expression for revelation and inspiration – for that interplay between events as the senses perceive them, and their meaning as the heart understands them. To be aware of the operation of grace is to recognize the divine creativity in events. Thus, for the religious person the whole of life is a series of operations of grace.

Friedrich Schleiermacher: On Religion

Genuine faith

When people talk about faith, they usually mean impressing someone else's thoughts and attitudes onto one's own mind. They claim that such faith is the very apex of religion. But in reality it is a betrayal of truth and an enslavement of the heart. It is nothing but an echo; it should be spurned by anyone wanting to enter the real sanctuary of religion.

Genuine faith consists in knowing oneself to be in possession of religion. True faith involves no loss of intellectual honesty, and no emotional slavery. On the contrary, it is a place where you can be entirely honest with yourself, and where you can be yourself. Indeed, the desire to be yourself is the beginning of faith.

Friedrich Schleiermacher: On Religion

CHRISTIAN MYSTICISM

Jesus spoke of his personal relationship with God as Father, and many Christians have aspired to a direct, mystical encounter. Gregory of Nyssa (d. c. 394) regarded the beauty of God's creation as a revelation of God. John Climacus (d. 650), who lived as hermit on Mount Sinai, used the ladder as a metaphor of the soul's ascent to God. Isaac the Syrian taught that the purpose of prayer is to carry the soul beyond prayer. Symeon of Galatia (d.1022), a monk who refused the offer of an archbishopric, experienced God as inner light.

Hildegaard of Bingen (d. 1179), an abbess who was also a musician and physician, taught people to seek God in all living creatures. Hadewijch of Brabant (d.c. 1240) described mystical union with God in physical terms. Jan van Ruusbroec (d. 1381) and Johann Tauler (d. 1361) were the two most celebrated teachers of mysticism in medieval Europe. Richard Rolle (d. 1349), a wandering bard, Julian of Norwich (d. 1416), an anchorite, and Walter Hilton (d. 1395), a hermit, were the most prominent figures in the flowering of mysticism in England. The writings of Thomas à Kempis (d.1471) are probably second only to the Bible as a source of inspiration among Christians. Teresa of Avila (d. 1582) and John of the Cross (d. 1591) in Spain, and Francis de Sales (d. 1622) in Geneva, were leaders in the spiritual renewal of Catholicism after the Protestant break with Rome. Angelus Silesius (d. 1677) in Germany, and Jean-Pierre de Caussade (d. 1751) in France, encouraged quiet serenity. Nikolaus von Zinzendorf (d. 1760) asserted the importance of spiritual experience above correct belief.

Discovering God's beauty

Fix your eyes on the infinite beauty of God. You will constantly discover the beauty anew. And it will constantly seem
strange, because it is different from what the mind normally
conceives. As you look upon God's beauty, he will continue
to reveal himself to you ever more fully. And, as he reveals
himself, your desire to see him will increase. You will sense
that the beauty you see now, is merely a hint of the glorious
beauty yet to be revealed.

   You may try to communicate with God in words, but
words can never encompass your relationship with him.
Some will tell you that the object of your love is unattainable
– that God can never be apprehended. At times the frustra-
tion of not being able to see God in his fullness will be so
great that you will feel spiritually beaten and wounded. But
you will come to realize that the true satisfaction of your desire consists in the quest for God, in never ceasing to ascend
towards him – and in desiring him ever more intensely.

Gregory of Nyssa: On the Song of Songs 12

Seeing God in creation

God in his essence, as he exists in himself, transcends all human knowledge. He cannot be approached or comprehended by intellectual speculation. Yet there is another way in which God can be apprehended; indeed, there are numerous ways.

We can apprehend him by inference through his wisdom reflected in the universe. Think of a human work of art: the mind can apprehend the artist in the artistry. But note that the mind does not see the essence of the artist, merely the skill that he has revealed in his work. Similarly, when we look at creation, we form an image not of the essence of the Creator, but of the wisdom he has revealed in his work.

Consider, for example, human life itself. God created human beings not out of any necessity, but by the goodness of his own free will. Thus, when we reflect on ourselves, we do not perceive God in himself, but we see his goodness. In the same way, we can see God's goodness in every object around us; and the contemplation of any object carries our minds upwards to the supreme source of goodness.

Gregory of Nyssa: On the Beatitudes 6

Darkness as enlightenment

Religious knowledge comes first to people as light. Thus it is perceived to be contrary to darkness; indeed, religion is seen as an escape from darkness. But as the soul progresses, and becomes more vibrant, it comes to realize how little of God it truly perceives; it recognizes that in truth in remains in darkness.

Indeed, the darkness that comes from spiritual progress is far more profound than natural darkness. The soul leaves behind all natural light, because it becomes indifferent to the things of nature; and in this darkness it becomes aware of its ignorance of God. It thus yearns for God. Eventually the yearning leads to an indirect knowledge of God. The soul becomes aware that seeing God consists in not seeing, because knowledge of God transcends all knowledge. The soul is thus surrounded on every side by darkness; yet the darkness is now a source of enlightenment.

Gregory of Nyssa: Life of Moses 162, 163

The soul's exertion

There is nothing to break the impetus of the soul. The nature of goodness is that it always aspires to do better. In the same way, the nature of the soul is that it always reaches upwards, yearning for the supreme goodness of heaven. The soul never becomes weary of climbing new and higher summits; each summit gives the soul fresh energy to climb the next summit. This is because spiritual activity has the special attribute of nurturing its own strength as it exerts it. Thus, as the soul climbs higher it acquires the ability to climb higher still.

Gregory of Nyssa: Life of Moses 225, 226

Inner and outer peace

You must never allow hostility to rise up in your heart; it must be killed absolutely and permanently. You should never give way to anger, or nurse grudges, because this would threaten your soul. And, above all, you must never act on these feelings, as this would only fan them into a greater blaze.

We bear the name of Christ, who is peace. For this reason we are called to put an end to all hostility. In every situation where people are divided, Christ can break down the wall that divides them, and make peace. Thus, when people attack you, then you should, through prayer, invite Christ to reconcile you with your attacker. But you can only do this if you yourself are free from all hostile feelings. Once you have attained this freedom, the spirit and the flesh are no longer in conflict.

In short, when you are at peace within yourself, then Christ can work through you to make peace with others.

Gregory of Nyssa: A Treatise on Perfection

Salvation for all

God is the life of all free beings. He is the salvation of all: of believers and unbelievers; of the just and the unjust; of the devout and those who ignore religion; of those free from evil passions and those enslaved by them; of monks and those living in the world; of the educated and the illiterate; of the healthy and the sick; of the young and the old. He is like the light and the heat of the sun, and the changes in the weather, which are the same for everyone.

Those who know God's salvation, strive to live in communion with his creation, and thus be free from sin. They take every opportunity to do good. They are self-controlled, holding fast to God amid the trials, snares and noise of the world. They rise above all difficulties.

John Climacus: *Ladder of Divine Ascent* 1

Perfection for all

Those who are married, can attain the same state of perfection as monks. They should be generous. They should speak evil of no one, rob no one and tell no lies. They should despise no one, and never carry hatred. They should not imagine themselves spiritually superior to anyone. They should show compassion to the needy. They should not intentionally cause offence to anyone. They should be satisfied with their lot.

To cultivate perfection is hard and the quest for perfection can often seem like a terrible burden. But a moment comes when the sense of burden lifts, and a flame of joy lights in the heart.

John Climacus: *Ladder of Divine Ascent* 1

Sincere repentance

Repentance is the renewal of your contract with God, giving you a fresh start. Repentance goes into the spiritual market-place, and tries to purchase humility. Repentance distrusts excessive bodily comfort. Repentance means standing on a watchtower, keeping guard over yourself. Repentance is the daughter of hope, and the son of the refusal to despair. Repentance means acknowledging guilt, and yet not being disgraced.

Those who take pride in their repentance, and who congratulate themselves on their tears of remorse, are like a man who asks his king for a weapon against an enemy – and then turns it on himself.

When people sincerely repent, God does not want them to continue weeping with remorse. He wants them to rejoice that they are reunited with him. He wants their souls to rejoice. After all, if the sin has been taken away, tears are superfluous. Why look for a bandage when the wound has already healed?

When you die, you will not be criticized for having failed to work miracles. You will not be accused of having failed to understand theology. But you will certainly be rebuked if you have not frequently repented.

John Climacus: *Ladder of Divine Ascent* 5, 7

Body and voice in prayer

In the early stages of prayer, bodily movements and postures can be very helpful. These include stretching out the hands, beating the breast, raising the eyes towards heaven, deep sighs, and even lying down face downwards. But this is not always feasible when other people are present.

So, if you can, go somewhere private in order to pray. Try to raise the eyes of your soul – to assist your spiritual eyes – by lifting your arms over your body in the shape of a cross. Then cry out to God, who has the power to serve you. Do not bother with elegant and clever words. Just say repeatedly: 'Have mercy on me, for I am a sinner.'

John Climacus: Ladder of Divine Ascent 15

Enjoying and describing humility

Do you imagine that words can precisely, or truly, or appropriately, or clearly, or honestly describe the divine joy that humility brings. Can words express the purity, the enlightenment, the wonder and the serenity that comes from a humble heart? Could you ever convey these things to someone who has not experienced them? It would be like using words and metaphors to convey the sweetness of honey to people who had never tasted it.

One person says: 'Humility is forgetting your own achievements.' Another says: 'Humility is regarding yourself as the least important person in the world and the greatest sinner.' A third person says: 'Humility is awareness of your own weakness and vulnerability.' A fourth says: 'Humility is being quick to end a quarrel by offering words of contrition.' A fifth says: 'Humility is the acknowledgement of divine grace and mercy.' A sixth says: 'Humility is an attitude of obedience in which you submit to God.' I have thought about all these definitions carefully and quietly. All seem correct, but none seems complete. Like a dog gathering crumbs from a table, I put these wise words together, and say: 'Humility is a gift from God, of indescribable beauty and immeasurable value. Its name is known only to those who have experienced it.'

John Climacus: *Ladder of Divine Ascent* 25

Sweetness and vision

The sweetness of prayer is one thing; and the divine vision, that is the ultimate fruit of prayer, is another thing. Just as an immature child turns into a mature adult, so the sweetness of prayer is the prelude to the divine vision.

Sometimes a verse from the Bible or a hymn becomes sweet in your mouth. You find yourself repeating it over and over again, not tiring of it, so that you are unable to move onto the next verse. This repetitive prayer may lead to a divine vision – and then the repetition is suddenly cut short. You feel as though the breath is leaving your body, so you are unable to speak.

This divine vision is not some image or form; it is not a picture in the mind. But it still has distinctive features. This is because you are still praying; you are still active. You have not transcended prayer; you have not risen to the spiritual place where there is no prayer. Your heart is still moving; you are not yet in the secret chamber, where the heart becomes utterly still.

Isaac the Syrian: Homily 23

Pure prayer

Just as the laws and commandments ordained by God are aimed at purifying the heart, so every form and mode of prayer is aimed at purifying the soul – and hence leads to pure prayer. Sighs, protestations, heartfelt supplications, cries of repentance, and every other expression to God, help to prepare the soul for pure prayer.

But a moment comes when the soul crosses the boundary from these active forms of prayer into the realm of pure prayer. At that moment active prayer ceases, so does activity of every kind and so do both physical and spiritual desire. When the soul enters pure prayer, it ceases to pray. Before entering this realm prayer is a constant struggle, in which the soul strives to gain authority over wayward thoughts and feelings. Beyond this boundary prayer is replaced by awestruck wonder, in which the soul marvels at the beauty of God.

You may ask why this motionless communion with God is called prayer, if it is not prayer. The reason is that prayer is the means by which the soul attains such a state. There is no other way of reaching it except through prayer. The soul is led by prayer towards it; prayer prepares the soul to receive it and it occurs during prayer. While you pray, you are concentrating on God; in every moment of prayer the soul is reaching out to God; in prayer the soul is opening itself to God with eager longing.

Isaac the Syrian: Homily 23

The spiritual fire

When you practise self-discipline, when you mount the steps of repentance, a gift comes down upon you from heaven: you taste the sweetness of spiritual knowledge. You become certain that God loves and provides for every person and every creature on earth. You are filled with wonder at the gracious way in which he governs the world. Gradually the sweetness turns into a spiritual fire, that burns within your heart, and spreads throughout your soul and body. You feel a passionate love for every person and every creature you encounter. You become drunk with love, as if you had been imbibing the finest wine. Your limbs grow limp, and your mind stands still in awestruck wonder. Your heart is captivated by God. Your inner senses grow strong, and you can begin to see God himself, as he is.

This experience is open to all those who struggle to lead righteous lives, who are vigilant in their care for others, and who devote much time to spiritual reading and to prayer. Gradually God's power takes hold of the soul. And when this experience occurs, you forget yourself; although you remain within the body, you become utterly unaware of yourself as a distinct individual.

Isaac the Syrian: Homily 49

The seed of truth

Once this spiritual fire has consumed you, then the soul begins to grow and deepen in its understanding of the hidden mysteries of God. The soul transcends the body, and is no longer constrained by bodily needs and feelings. It is thus free to receive every kind of revelation that the Spirit of God can give.

It is as if a seed has been planted in the soul; and the warmth of the spiritual fire has caused the seed to rise up and thrive, bearing spiritual fruit in the form of heavenly knowledge. Indeed, this seed is present in every soul from the moment of birth. But most people are so distracted by vain concerns, by transient and fleeting pleasures, that they are never aware of it; so it remains dormant. Blessed are those who recognize the seed within their souls, and nurture it.

Isaac the Syrian: Homily 49

Starting to pray

When you start to pray, come before God like a baby who
has not yet learnt to talk. Do not try to speak to God at first;
and do not show off any theological knowledge you may
have. All the thoughts in your mind should be those of a
child. Look upon God as a child looks upon a father or
mother, in a spirit of total trust.

A central part of learning to pray is repentance. Allow
yourself to weep over your sins. Only when you reach the
plane of tears does your soul begin to emerge from the prison
of this world, and set foot on the path of freedom – the freedom of 'pure prayer'. As you breathe the air outside the
prison, your tears of sorrow become tears of joyful relief. You
are like a baby emerging from the womb at birth; the process
of birth is an intense struggle, and the relief at the end of the
process is equally intense. Your mother is divine grace, who
wants to bring every soul on earth to spiritual birth. Just as a
baby suddenly starts breathing air, and can sense all the smells
that the air carries, so, as you come to spiritual birth, you can
smell a sweet fragrance – a spiritual fragrance that suggests
the ecstatic bliss that awaits you.

Isaac the Syrian: Homily 117

Attaining God's light

Let no one deceive you. God is light; and those who have entered into union with him, experience great inward brightness. The mind, which is the lamp of the soul, is lit by the divine fire, and bursts into flame. It is a miracle. By this means your body too is heated. Thus the body, mind and soul are united with God. Just as the mind cannot be separated from the soul, neither can the body; the whole person becomes joined to God, sharing his eternal life.

How, then, do we attain God's light? How can we run towards his brightness? The path to his light leads by way of repentance. Do not be frightened of repenting your sins. His light is so strong that it illuminates your footsteps as you tread this path. But you must hurry; you must run while there is still time. You must repent before the darkness of death overtakes you. When you have reached the place of repentance, allow yourself to weep; your tears are an acknowledgement of your sin. And as you weep, the Lord will fulfil his promise of mercy. He will forgive you.

God wants us to run the path of his kingdom, and to knock on the door of heaven, while we are still on earth. If we refuse to go to his kingdom while we are alive, why should he let us in when we die?

Symeon of Galatia: The Discourses 15

Filled with joy

One night, when I was still a young man, I went to the place where I usually prayed. As usual I opened my heart to God. But on this occasion I was suddenly moved to tears, and my whole body and soul were seized with desire for God. At first I thought that my tears were from sadness; then I realized that I was filled with joy and pleasure. I fell prostrate to the ground, and at once I saw a huge light. It shone upon me, penetrating my mind and soul. I was utterly amazed and overcome with ecstasy. I became quite oblivious of where I was, or even who I was. I could only cry out: 'Lord, have mercy.'

Eventually I returned to my normal state, and found myself still reciting: 'Lord have mercy.' I began to reflect on my experience and ask questions. Who was moving my tongue? Was I inside or outside my body when I saw the light? God alone knows the answers. But I knew that my experience had changed me. It had scattered the mist of my soul, and cast out every earthly care. It made my body light, so that my limbs no longer felt sluggish and heavy. My muscles were strengthened and invigorated. My mind was stripped of its garment of corruption. And my soul had a sensation of sweetness, greater than that of the sweetest food. My thoughts were directed entirely towards the things of heaven, and I no longer felt any fear of death. My mind and my soul were wholly absorbed in the ineffable joy of that light.

Symeon of Galatia: Discourses 16

Symbols of heaven

After a time the light which I had seen faded and disappeared. I felt utterly alone, and I was gripped by a pain and a grief so great that I cannot describe it. It was like a fire consuming my heart. It seemed to me that the fire had represented the infinite love of God, which had wholly captivated my emotions, and now I was separated from this love. So I went to seek advice from the old man who was my spiritual guide.

He said to me: 'The light, and the experiences which accompany it, are only symbols of heaven, not heaven itself; they are a foretaste of the bliss of heaven. You will not taste heaven itself while you are still alive on this earth. In the meantime you should do nothing that can hinder you from eventually entering heaven. Undoubtedly you will fall from time to time, committing some sin. Do not despair; those occasional lapses ensure that you remain humble. So continue to cultivate a spirit of repentance, knowing that God alone can blot out past and present failures.'

When I heard these words, I felt a wonderful sense of relief. I recognized that this old man spoke from a great height of spiritual knowledge; and he had acquired that knowledge because he trusted God without reserve.

Symeon of Galatia: Discourses 16

The power of love

Once I had started on the path, I became obsessed with fear;
I felt that evil forces were trying to attack and destroy me. Yet
in fact the warfare was provoked not by evil, but by love; the
power of love had entered my soul, and was attacking the evil
that had always lurked there. Sinful habits were deeply rooted
within me, so the battle between love and evil was fierce and
long. But when I recognized the true nature of the battle, I
joined forces with love by imposing on myself a strict dis-
cipline of prayer and constant meditation on the New
Testament.

Symeon of Galatia: Discourses 17

Understanding creation

Use all your faculties to appreciate God's creation. Use your soul to understand other souls. Use your body to sympathize with other people's bodily experiences. Use your emotions of anger and revenge to understand war. Appreciate goodness through distinguishing it from evil. Appreciate beauty through distinguishing it from ugliness and deformity. Define poverty by contrasting it with wealth. Rejoice in good health by comparing it with sickness.

Distinguish the various opposites: length and shortness; hardness and softness; depth and shallowness; light and darkness. Enjoy every moment of life by constantly reminding yourself of the imminence of death. Look forward to paradise by reminding yourself of eternal punishment.

You understand so little of what is around you, because you do not use what is within you.

Hildegard of Bingen: Scivias I

God's sound, goodness and breathing

The power of God is known through all the various species of plants and animals in the world, which have been created by the Word of God. As the honesty of a person is known through the value of that person's word, so the holiness and goodness of the Creator is known through the value of the Creator's Word. And that value is made manifest through the creation.

A word that is spoken, has three elements: sound, goodness and breathing. A word has sound in order to be heard, goodness in order to be understood and breathing in order that it may be completed. So too with God. The creation is God's sound, by which he enables all to perceive his power and glory. The coming of Christ is God's goodness, which prompts him to become a human being. And the Holy Spirit is God's breathing, by which he enters all people.

Hildegard of Bingen: Scivias 2

God's power and beauty

God is shown through the Word; the Word is shown through the creation of the world and all the species that inhabit it; and the Holy Spirit is shown through the Word being made flesh. What does this mean? God is the one who brought the Word into being before the beginning of time. The Word is the one through whom all creatures are made. The Holy Spirit is the one who enters creation at particular moments.

The Word of God is shown through the power of God in creating the world. The Word called into being from nothing all the different species that inhabit the world. These species all shine with beauty, reflecting the beauty of their origins. They sparkle in the beauty of their perfection, as if they had all been made of burnished copper. Their light shines in every direction, so the whole earth glows with beauty.

When you see God's beauty, you are not looking with mortal eyes, but with the eyes of the soul. When you hear his Word, you are not using mortal ears, but listening with the ears of your soul to the wisdom he has implanted within you.

Hildegard of Bingen: Scivias 2

Holiness and rebellion

The Word of God is burning love. The Word brings life to those who are dead in soul. The Word is a light that exposes sin, and a flame that burns the ropes binding sin to the soul. The Word exists in every person before the person is aware of the Word. The Word is the source of holiness in each person, and makes people desire to become holy. The Word is magnificent and glorious, and can never be comprehended by the human intellect.

Imagine the highest and widest mountain in the world. Its size reflects the grandeur of God, and thus honours God. It is not greater than God; nothing on earth is greater than its Creator. God is higher and wider than the human mind can comprehend. He is holier than we could possibly understand. No creatures can attain the holiness of God, because God is above all creatures. Yet human beings, alone among the creatures on earth, are reluctant to honour God. They claim that it is difficult and tedious to worship God; they feel too weak to praise him. Every human being is a rebel against God.

Hildegard of Bingen: Scivias 3

Openness to God

Those who love God, open themselves entirely to him. They ask him to enter their senses, their souls and their minds. They receive him with joy; they embrace him with every thought and feeling; they want to perceive him with all their senses. And God rejoices in them, regarding them as more fragrant than the most fragrant flower in creation, as brighter than the brightest jewel, as nobler than the noblest mountain. And he wants to make them sweeter in smell, even more sparkling, and yet more handsome.

He feasts their minds with delicious thoughts, and he presses his justice into their hearts. He gives them the sweetest spiritual water to refresh their souls. Yet sometimes he seems to abandon them, so that they find themselves without his help. He does this so they do not become puffed up with spiritual pride. They weep and moan, and may even become angry with God. In this way their faith is tested.

Hildegard of Bingen: Scivias 3

The humanity of God

All of us want to live with God in comfort, enjoying his spiritual treasures and sharing in the pleasure of his glory. We all
want to be gods with God. But God alone knows how few of
us want to live as humans with his humanity, to carry his
cross with him, and to be crucified with him in order to pay
the price for the world's sins.

When we live on earth with the humanity of God, we experience suffering and distress, while rejoicing inwardly in
the sweet love of the almighty and eternal Godhead. These are
two sides of a single experience. And just as Jesus Christ on
earth submitted to the will of the majestic Father, so we too
should submit lovingly to the Father and the Son. We should
serve them in humility, following their commands in every
aspect of our lives. Let them do with us whatever they want.

We should not hold back anything from God. We should
work for God with ready and faithful hands, practising every
kind of virtue. And we should not love the Godhead with
devotion alone, but with desires so deep that they cannot be
expressed or described. God's love will then explode into our
lives, lifting us out of ourselves so that we are brought into
spiritual unity with God. It will no longer be an obligation
and duty to serve God, but a joy and privilege, undertaken
with inexhaustible vigour. Our goal will be to ensure that
God's love takes its rightful place in the lives of all people and
all creatures – to ensure that the whole world dies with Christ
on the cross, and rises with him to new life.

Hadewijch of Brabant: Letters 6

True love

Those who truly love God and their neighbours, are bound to renounce all worldly ambitions, and to renounce too all pride in their own abilities and achievements. Their only desire is to know the source of love.

Those who truly love God and their neighbours, rejoice in being corrected by others. They do not try to excuse their own mistakes; rather they eagerly learn how to follow God more closely.

Those who truly love God and their neighbours, are willing to endure anything for the sake of love. They happily accept insults and blows in the pursuit of love.

Those who truly love God and their neighbours, are equally happy in company or alone, as love requires.

Hadewijch of Brabant: Letters 8

Permeated by God

May God make known to you who he is, and how he treats his servants – how he draws them into himself. From the depths of his wisdom he will teach you about his love. He will live in you, and you will live in him, so that you will taste his wonderful sweetness.

You will be like two lovers. You will be so besotted with God, that you will not know where your own self ends, and where God begins. It will seem as if you and God possess one another in mutual delight, mouth in mouth, heart in heart, body in body, soul in soul. The divine nature will flow into you, permeating you.

You will find yourself by finding God.

Hadewijch of Brabant: Letters 9

The measure of love

Those who truly love God, also love his works. The works of God are expressions of supreme virtue. Therefore those who love God, also love virtue.

The love of virtue brings great joy and strength. Acting virtuously is the clearest demonstration of love. Indeed, virtuous action is a better proof of love than religious observance, or the sweetness that often accompanies religious observance. People may be devout in their religion, and gain great pleasure from it, yet be empty of love. The measure of love lies not in our feelings, but in the degree to which we serve others.

Hadewijch of Brabant: Letters 10

Self-knowledge

If you want to be perfect, you must first know yourself. You must understand what you are able to do, and what you are willing to do; what you love, and what you hate; what you trust, and what you distrust; and how you react emotionally to events. You have to reflect on how you respond to people opposing you, and how you cope in unfamiliar surroundings.

You have to ask yourself how you endure the loss of things you like. And you have to examine whether you rise quickly and eagerly to opportunities for good. As you understand yourself, so you will be able to control yourself, remaining serene and tranquil in all circumstances. Thus, you will be able to remain constantly close to God — and perfection.

Hadewijch of Brabant: Letters 14

The essence of the soul

Now we must inquire into the deepest essence of the soul – what the soul is. The soul is an essence which is transparent to God, and to which God is transparent. Indeed, the soul is more than this; it is an essence that wants to give delight to God. The soul is a divine essence, which retains its divine qualities so long as it does not become enmeshed in things that are alien to it.

If the soul remains true to itself, it becomes a receptacle of the infinite dimensions into which God can enter, and in which God can receive and bestow great joy. The soul is the path by which God enters human beings; the soul is God's home on earth. So long as God is not completely filling the soul, then the soul is not satisfied.

Hadewijch of Brabant: Letters 18

Obedience and pride

To be obedient is to deny your own will in deference to
God's will. It is quite possible to act in a good and virtuous
manner, and yet still to be self-willed.

Obedience means no longer deciding what actions should
be performed, and what actions should be avoided. It means
no longer deciding what hardships should be endured, and
what may be escaped. In this way pride is banished, and
humility is nurtured and made perfect. God becomes master
of the will; and the will becomes so united to God that the
individual desires nothing else apart from this unity.

Jan van Ruusbroec: Spiritual Espousals 125

The touch of God

The grace of God, which flows from God, is an interior impulse or prompting. It comes through the Holy Spirit, and directs your spirit from within, guiding your actions in the way of virtue. This grace is inside you, not outside, for God is more interior to you than you are to yourself; and he is closer to you and more intimate than your own thoughts and feelings. Thus God starts inside you and works outward; whereas all other influences start outside you and work inward.

The touch of God occurs when the grace of God floods into the soul like a mighty river; or when it burns into the soul like a blazing fire; or when it bubbles up from within the soul like a spring; or when it appears like a plant with its roots embedded firmly within the soul. You receive the touch of God passively and it brings all the disparate powers of the soul into unity.

God alone is active; he alone is the cause of this blessing. You cannot explain what is happening; you cannot describe the divine love that you feel; you cannot understand the manner of God's touch, or what it comprises. This touch is the source of all graces and all gifts; and it is the last intermediary between God and the soul.

Jan van Ruusbroec: Spiritual Espousals 147, 196

Penetrating the door

Those who through contemplation have reached down to the depths of their own souls, and thence come to the door of eternal life, are able to feel the touch of God. The radiance is so great that all the intellectual powers of the mind fail, and cannot go onward; the mind must remain outside the door. Only love can penetrate further, and go through the door, because love has no wish to understand God; it wants only to enjoy him. Love desires to taste and savour God, not to analyze him. That is why love can go in, while the mind stops outside.

Jan van Ruusbroec: Spiritual Espousals 198

Pure intentions

You can meet God in all your activities, becoming more like him, and growing closer to him in blissful love. Every good work, however small it may be, which is undertaken out of love for God, with a pure and righteous intention, renews you in his image and prepares you for eternal life in him. A pure intention unites the diverse powers of the soul in harmony, and directs the soul towards God.

A pure intention is the source and purpose of virtue, and is a thing of beauty. A pure intention is an act of praise to God, honouring his name. A pure intention transcends itself, carrying the soul upwards to heaven. An intention is pure if God is its origin, and if it sees all things in relation to God.

When your intentions are pure, the powers of the soul are brought into harmony. You offer your whole life to God, and you encounter him in every virtuous act. Indeed, your actions become his actions. Thus, on the foundation of pure intentions you transcend yourself, and you meet God without any intermediary. You rest in his presence, and there take possession of the inheritance that has been preserved for you for all eternity.

Jan van Ruusbroec: Spiritual Espousals 209, 210

Mystical union

Sometimes those who live the interior life, are drawn into themselves. They disengage themselves from outward virtues and activities, and find within their own soul the source of love. They meet God without any intermediary; and, as they gaze on him, they experience perfect bliss. They perceive a light that comes from the depths of God's unity; and beyond this light they see only darkness, emptiness, nothingness.

To outward appearances these people seem to be enveloped in darkness; they are dead to the world. But inwardly they are basking in God's radiance. Outwardly all life seems to have drained away from them; inwardly they are overwhelmed by the vibrant love of God, which lasts forever. The divine essence permeates their souls; and in union with God they are in ecstasy.

Jan van Ruusbroec: Spiritual Espousals 223

The act of conversion

Your purpose is that God should be born within the soul. This requires a decisive act of conversion, in which all your powers and faculties, from the lowest to the highest, are directed towards God. It requires a gathering of the whole self, taking away every aspect of the self from worldly distractions, and placing the self in the arms of God. In this way the different aspects of the self no longer conflict with one another, but are brought into harmony.

The act of conversion may be compared with an archer who wants to hit the middle of the target, and closes one eye in order that the other eye can see clearly. In the same way conversion requires total and accurate attention onto the soul, which is the location of divine truth, and this means becoming blind to all else. The act of conversion may also be compared with a tree, in which the sap ceases to flow from the trunk to the branches, but flows back into the trunk. In the same way conversion requires all energy and all life to flow back into the soul, which is the source of life.

Through the act of conversion you are raised above and beyond yourself. You remove all selfish intentions, desires and actions, and strive for God alone. You cease to exist as an individual within yourself; you belong to him; he is so close to you that you no longer distinguish between yourself and him. This is what is meant by God being born within the soul: the seed of God was always there, but now you no longer hinder the seed's growth – so God flourishes within the soul.

Johann Tauler: Sermon 1

Peace in the absence of peace

There are many people who wish to be witnesses of God when their souls feel peaceful, and when their religious observance is giving pleasure. These people want to be holy, so long as their religious efforts do not become burdensome. But when darkness comes, when God seems remote and distant, when they feel lonely and abandoned, when their minds or bodies become sick – then they turn away from God, and show themselves not to be his true witnesses.

It is natural for all of us to seek peace, both in what we do, and in what we are. The true witnesses of God learn to find peace where peace is absent. This is because they are not concerned for peace in itself, but want to discover the source of peace – which is God. They learn to find joy in grief, serenity in disturbance, consolation in bitterness.

Johann Tauler: Sermon 21

The soul's hidden chamber

Within the soul there exists a hidden chamber which is outside time and space, and which transcends that part of the soul giving life and movement to the body. It is within this hidden chamber that we encounter divinity; it is there that we become utterly still, totally true to ourselves, completely detached from all material concerns.

The atmosphere within that chamber is pure; within that chamber you are free from all bonds. God dwells, acts and rules within that chamber. Entering that chamber cannot be compared with any other aspect of your life, even the most devout religious observance. There you are united with God; there the fire of his love burns, and you are consumed by it.

Johann Tauler: Sermon 24

Becoming perfect

If you want to become perfect and to fulfil your spiritual potential, you must bear two points in mind. First, you should free your heart from all material and worldly things; you must even free your heart from any concerns about yourself.

Secondly, you must accept all difficulties – whatever their cause, whether they are material or spiritual – as coming from God. In this way you will learn to submit yourself to God, giving yourself totally to him; and he in turn will be able to bestow the full riches of his spiritual gifts upon you.

Johann Tauler: Sermon 25

God and the self

Two beings, two entities, cannot occupy the same space. If warmth enters a space, then cold must leave. In the same way, God and the self cannot both occupy your soul. If God is to enter your soul, then the self must leave.

This means that, if God is to be born within your soul, you must cease to assert yourself, and become totally passive. All your faculties must be stripped of their power of action; you must suppress your will; your pride must evaporate into the air. The more you become nothing, the more God will grow in your soul.

Johann Tauler: Sermon 31

The fire of love

I cannot describe to you how astonished I was the first time I felt my heart begin to warm. The warmth was real, not imaginary; it seemed as if I were actually on fire. I was amazed at the way the heat surged through me; and this sensation gave me great pleasure and comfort – which surprised me also. I kept touching my chest, to convince myself that there was no physical cause.

Once I was sure that this fire of love was not the result of some illness, bodily or mental, but was a gift from my Maker, I was utterly delighted, and I wished the fire to burn ever brighter. And the desire was enhanced by the wonderful inner sweetness I could taste as the fire blazed. I had never imagined that sinful human beings could enjoy such spiritual warmth and sweetness.

Richard Rolle: Fire of Love, Prologue

Holy and carnal flames

No one could survive this fire if it continued to burn fiercely; the body and the soul would wilt in the face of such intense heat. Yet once you have experienced the heat, and the sweetness that accompanies it, you desire nothing else; with every breath you long for the heat and the sweetness to occur. Indeed, you want to quit this world, in order to enjoy permanently this honeyed flame in heaven.

Yet while you remain in this world, feelings often rise up in the heart that compete with this flame. Carnal desires and affections continue to blaze from time to time. This sinful fire cannot take away the holy fire; once the holy fire has started to burn, it cannot be extinguished. But the carnal fire can seduce you into ignoring it; and the holy flames die down, so that you become spiritually frozen. Thus it is vital that you continually remind yourself about the holy fire, and rekindle it.

Richard Rolle: Fire of Love, Prologue

Warmth, sweetness and song

I have found that to love Christ has three effects: warmth, melody and sweetness. And I know from my own experience that these cannot persist for long without bringing great inner stillness and silence.

These three things are signs of pure love; they are tokens of the spiritual perfection that is found in the Christian religion. To the limits of my meagre nature I have received them, as a gift from Jesus.

I dare not compare myself with the saints who have experienced these things, because they received them far more fully. But I shall continue trying to grow in virtue, so that my love burns more fervently, my song becomes sweeter, and I taste the sweetness of love more fully.

Richard Rolle: Fire of Love 14

The moment of change

I was sitting in church, trying to find pleasure in prayer and meditation, when suddenly I felt within me a strange and pleasant heat. At first I wondered where it came from, but gradually I realized that it did not have a natural cause; it came from the Creator himself. The warmth was extremely intense, and gave me great joy.

Nine months later a wonderful sensation of sweetness was added to the sensation of heat. And I also began to hear spiritual sounds, which seemed to fill the church. These sounds were hymns of eternal praise, sung to a heavenly melody which I had never heard on earth. Indeed, they cannot be heard except by those who have received them from above, and who have purified themselves from the things of this world.

That night, as I sat in church before supper reciting psalms, I heard above me again the sound of holy words being sung. With all my heart I was reaching out to heaven; and this symphony seemed to me, in a manner I cannot explain, to be heaven's response to me. And in my mind I felt myself to be in perfect and delightful harmony with the music.

Then and there my thoughts turned themselves into a heavenly melody, and my meditation became a poem; every prayer I uttered, and every psalm I recited, swelled this wonderful chorus. Through this inner sweetness my whole being began to sing; but I sang without any outward sound, so that only my Creator could hear.

Richard Rolle: Fire of Love 15

Creation in a hazelnut

Our Lord showed me something small, no bigger than a hazelnut. It seemed to lie in the palm of my hand, and was as round as a ball. I gazed on it with the eye of understanding, and thought: 'What can this be?'

I received the answer: 'It is all that is made.'

I marvelled that it could last; it was so small that I thought it would quickly disappear. And in my understanding I received a further answer: 'It lasts, and will last forever, because God loves it; all things exist through the love of God.'

In this little thing I saw three properties. The first is that God made it; the second is that God loves it; the third is that God preserves it. I saw in it that God is creator, lover, and preserver. And until I am wholly united with him, I can never enjoy true rest or true happiness. I must become attached to him in such a way that nothing stands between me and him.

The little thing seemed to me so small that it could have faded into nothing. We should despise nothing that God has created, and delight in everything. By this means we love and understand the uncreated God.

Julian of Norwich: *Divine Showings* 5

The necessity of sin

I saw nothing hindered me except sin. This is true for all of us. And it seemed to me that if there had been no sin, we should all have been pure, just as the Lord created us. Indeed, prior to this time I often used to wonder, in my folly, why God in his great and prophetic wisdom had not prevented sin from ever existing. If sin did not exist, it seemed to me that all would be well.

These thoughts should have been suppressed. But lacking insight, I felt deeply sad and sorrowful at the existence of sin. Jesus in a vision told me what I needed to know about this. He said: 'Sin is necessary. But all will be well, and all will be well, and every kind of thing will be well.'

It is true that sin is the cause of pain. But all will be well, and every kind of thing will be well. These words were spoken most tenderly, showing that no blame attached to me or to anyone who will be saved. Thus it would be quite wrong for me to blame God for sin, or to criticize him for letting me sin, since he does not blame me.

Julian of Norwich: Divine Showings 27

The necessity of pain

I saw that the Lord rejoices, with pity and compassion, over
the tribulations of his servants. And on every person whom
he loves, he imposes some burden. This burden is not a de-
fect in his sight, but is an aid to the attainment of eternal
bliss. It may cause a person to be humiliated and despised in
this world – to be scorned, mocked and rejected. The Lord
does this to prevent the damage which comes from hubris,
pride and self-importance in this wretched life, and thus to
prepare the soul for the eternal, everlasting bliss of heaven.
The Lord says: 'I shall completely break down within you
empty ambition and vanity. And I shall gather you in my
arms to make you meek and mild, pure and holy.'

Julian of Norwich: *Divine Showings* 28

Divine motherhood

The natural mother can give her child milk from her breasts. Our spiritual mother Jesus can feed us with himself with great dignity and tenderness. He feeds us through his most merciful actions and gracious words.

This beautiful and enchanting word 'mother' is so sweet and alluring that it cannot be truly applied to anyone except the one who is the mother of all creation. To motherhood belongs life, love, wisdom and knowledge; and these are properties of God. Certainly our physical birth is a simple and insignificant event compared with our spiritual birth. But the natural mother, who brings a child physically to birth, is guided and strengthened by the spiritual mother of all births.

The kind and loving natural mother knows and understands her infant well; and out of natural instinct she protects and provides for her infant. As the infant grows and develops, she acts differently; but her love does not change. She rebukes her child to deter misbehaviour, and to encourage virtue and grace. Everything which the natural mother does, is lovely and good. And the way our Lord treats us, his children, is the same. And for this reason we can call our Lord, 'Mother'.

Julian of Norwich: *Divine Showings* 60

Starting the pilgrimage

A real pilgrim going to Jerusalem leaves his house and land, his wife and children; he strips himself of all he possesses, in order to travel light. Similarly if you wish to be a spiritual pilgrim, you must strip yourself of all you possess. You must leave behind your bad deeds, and you must even leave behind your good deeds.

You must regard yourself as spiritually poor, so that you have no confidence in your own actions. Instead you should always desire the spiritual presence of Jesus, and his profound love. If you do this, your heart will be wholly set on reaching the spiritual Jerusalem – on obtaining the love of Jesus, and such vision of him as he sees fit to give you.

Walter Hilton: Ladder of Perfection 2.21

Enemies' attacks

You are now on the road, and you know the way. But beware of enemies who will try to obstruct you. They hate your desire and yearning for the love of Jesus; so they want to uproot this desire and yearning from your heart, and turn your heart back to worldly things. Your chief enemies are bodily desires and foolish fears, which can rise up in your heart and stifle your love of God, taking full possession of you. These are your deadliest foes.

There are other enemies also, who will use every trick to deceive you. But you have one sure means of resisting them. Whatever they say, do not believe them, but stride firmly onwards, thinking only of the love of Jesus. When they persist, say: 'I am nothing, I have nothing, I desire nothing, but the love of Jesus.'

Your enemies may begin by assailing your mind with doubts, hinting that you are not fit to enjoy God's love. 'Why do you yearn for something which you cannot possess and do not deserve?' they whisper. Do not be put off, but reply: 'I desire the love of God, not because I am worthy, but because I am unworthy – and I want it in order to become worthy. God created me to enjoy his love; and though I may never fully attain it, I shall still desire it, pray for it, and hope for it.'

Walter Hilton: Ladder of Perfection 2.22

Entering the darkness

Those who love God, live in his light. When people realize that the pleasures of this world are false and transitory, they want to abandon the world, and seek God's love. But they cannot experience God's love immediately; they must stay for some time in darkness. They cannot move instantly from one light to another, from the pleasures of this world to the perfect love of God.

This darkness is the complete withdrawal of the soul from worldly pleasures, motivated by an intense desire to love, see and know Jesus and the things of the spirit. It is a real night. The darkness of the natural night hides material objects and brings bodily activity to a halt; in the same way those who set their hearts on Jesus and his love, must hide all material desires from themselves.

Walter Hilton: Ladder of Perfection 2.24

The light of the heavenly city

You are now fast approaching Jerusalem. You have not yet arrived, but you can see the city in the distance because of the gleaming rays of light shining from it. Remember that, although your soul dwells in peaceful darkness, and is untroubled by thoughts of the world, it is not yet at the end of its journey. The soul has not yet been clothed in light, nor has it caught fire with divine love. The soul is still aware that the object of its ardent desire is beyond its reach. This object is nothing other than the vision of Jerusalem.

This city symbolizes the perfect love of God. The soul sees clearly that here is a reward transcending anything attainable by human effort. Thus the soul's only wish is to enter the city.

Walter Hilton: Ladder of Perfection 2.25

Imitating Christ

Christ urges us to mould our lives and our characters in the image of his – if we wish the light of truth to shine in our hearts. So above all else we should devote ourselves to meditating on the love of Jesus Christ.

The teaching of Jesus Christ is better than all the teachings of every holy and wise person that has ever lived; and anyone guided by the Spirit will find hidden nourishment there. Many people hear the gospel frequently, and yet feel little desire to imitate Christ. This is because they do not possess the Spirit of Christ. Those who wish to understand and savour the words of Christ in full, must ensure that their whole lives conform to the pattern of Christ's life.

Thomas à Kempis: Imitation of Christ 1. 1

The world of shadows

People may discuss theological doctrines with great skill; but, if they lack humility, they will displease God. Intellectual arguments do not make people holy and righteous; God wants us to lead good lives. I should rather feel repentance in my heart, than define it with my mind. You could know the entire Bible word for word, and be familiar with every exposition written by scholars; but, if you lacked the grace and love of God, the knowledge would be useless.

We live in a world of shadows. The only reality consists in loving God, and in serving him alone. The highest wisdom is to seek the kingdom of heaven, rejecting the things of this world. If you pursue riches, and believe they will make you happy, you are pursuing an empty fantasy. It is equally foolish to seek social status and honour, to become a slave to your natural appetites, to prefer a long life to a good life – to set your heart on anything in the world, which will soon pass away. Instead look only towards that place where lasting joy is to be found.

Thomas à Kempis: Imitation of Christ 1.1

The uselessness of knowledge

Human beings have a natural desire for knowledge. But what good is knowledge without love for God? Those who are humble and ignorant, and yet serve God with all their hearts, are better than proud scholars who observe the movements of the stars in the sky, yet never give a thought to their souls.

Those who really know themselves, set no value on themselves, and take no pleasure in being praised by others. Even if I were to know everything in the world, yet I lacked love, I should be worthless in the eyes of God.

So give up the passion for knowledge, which distracts you and leads you astray. Scholarly people like to be admired, and to acquire a reputation for wisdom.

But most knowledge does little or no good to the soul; and those who give their minds to things that do not contribute to salvation are fools. The soul can never be satisfied by words, even in their thousands; whereas a good life sets the mind at peace, and a pure conscience brings friendship with God.

Thomas à Kempis: Imitation of Christ 1.2

The uselessness of emotions

We are too concerned with our own emotions, and too concerned with the transitory objects of our emotions. We rarely try to overcome emotional faults, but merely offset their worst effects. Thus, we are not on fire to make progress. Yet if we had true control of our emotions, so that they were stripped of all transitory attachments, then we should be free to gain a glimpse of God, and to experience a taste of the joys of heavenly contemplation.

Thus, our emotional desires are our main and most intractable stumbling block, preventing us from fully imitating Christ. And it is not merely desires and attachments that hinder our progress; it is also the tendency for our emotions to be cast into a pit of gloom at the least adversity.

Let us learn to be firm with our emotions; and if we succeed in this, we shall find the path of Christ easy and delightful.

Thomas à Kempis: Imitation of Christ 1.11

Jesus as lover

If we disregard ourselves for the sake of Jesus, then we are truly blessed. If we abandon all other facets of love, and love Jesus above everything, then we are truly blessed. The love of other people is fickle and changeable, but the love of Jesus is consistent and enduring. Those who love material objects, will decay and crumble as those objects decay and crumble. But those who embrace Jesus, will be upheld forever.

When all else fades away, Jesus will still be present. Jesus never leaves us; he never lets us perish. Inevitably at some point in the future we shall each die, and shall have to leave all our possessions and all our earthly friends behind. But Jesus is with us in death, as in life. So keep close to Jesus, not only when you are healthy, but also when death approaches. Place all your trust in him, because he can always help you.

Jesus is a lover who tolerates no rivals. He wants to have your heart entirely to himself, and to rule there like a king. Thus, you must strip your heart of all attachments, so Jesus can possess your heart completely.

Thomas à Kempis: Imitation of Christ 2.7

Ecstatic prayer

In the highest stage of prayer the soul is conscious that it is fainting away in a kind of a swoon; it feels very calm, and full of joy. The breath and the bodily powers progressively fail, so that you cannot move even the hands without great effort. The eyes close involuntarily; and, if they remain open, they see almost nothing. If you try to read in such a state, you can scarcely make out a single letter – you can see that there are letters, but you cannot read them, even if you try. You hear, but you do not understand what you hear.

Your senses serve no purpose; you cannot even distinguish pleasure from pain. Your tongue cannot form a single word, nor would it have the strength to pronounce one. The strength of the body vanishes. As a result the strength of the soul increases, to enjoy its full bliss to the full.

This state of ecstatic prayer does no harm, however long it lasts. At least it has never harmed me. Even when I have been ill, I can never recall any bad effects from ecstatic prayer; on the contrary, it has always left me feeling much better. What harm could such a blessing do? The effects are so manifest that it is obvious to any observer that a wonderful thing is happening. At the time it robs you of your bodily strength; but afterwards you find your strength has increased.

In fact ecstatic prayer usually lasts only a very short time. It is so quick that the external signs are not always noticed by others. But once it is over, you are so radiant that it seems the sun is shining from your soul.

Teresa of Avila: Autobiography 18

The rising of the soul and body

In ecstatic prayer the Lord catches the soul, just as the clouds gather up the morning mists on earth; and the Lord carries the soul right out of itself, just as the clouds – so I am told – carry the mist towards the sun. The Lord takes the soul in the direction of heaven, to show the kingdom that he has prepared. I do not know whether this happens literally, but this is how it seems. In these raptures the soul no longer seems to be in the body; and the body's heat diminishes, so the flesh grows cold.

When the Lord begins to carry the soul upwards, at first you feel afraid; so this level of prayer requires great determination and courage. You must risk everything, and put yourself entirely in God's hands. You must allow yourself to be carried wherever God wants to take you. You might try to resist, and use all your strength to do so. In fact I myself sometimes want to resist, especially when I am in a public place, because I feel worried about causing embarrassment to others; I have even resisted in private because I am afraid that the experience is delusory. At times my struggle has been successful but it has been like fighting a great giant, leaving me utterly exhausted. At other times resistance has proved impossible; my soul has been carried away, and usually my mind as well, without my being able to stop them. Occasionally my entire body has been lifted off the ground.

Teresa of Avila: Autobiography 20

The purpose of ecstatic prayer

We may speak of love and humility as the true flowers of spiritual growth; and they give off a wonderful scent, which benefits all who come near. The purpose of ecstatic prayer is to enable these flowers to bloom.

Unless you have experienced ecstatic prayer, you can never imagine how much the Lord can accomplish through it, in such a short time. Of course, ecstatic prayer is not essential for spiritual growth; people who over many years follow the rules and principles of prayer, given by spiritual writers over the centuries, will eventually bear these beautiful flowers. But it is hard work, and takes much time. In ecstatic prayer, without any effort, the Lord raises the soul from the earth and lifts it to heaven.

The souls that receive the gift of ecstatic prayer, are not more deserving than those who do not. Certainly my soul has not merited this gift. The Lord bestows the gift of ecstatic prayer according to his pleasure. No soul is ever prepared for it; but God makes the soul ready as and when he wishes.

Teresa of Avila: Autobiography 21

An erotic vision

In a state of ecstatic prayer I once saw an angel. He was not tall, but short and very beautiful. His face glowed like a fire.

In his hands I saw a great golden spear, and the iron tip seemed to be burning. He plunged the spear into my heart several times, so deeply that it penetrated my entire body. Then, as he pulled the spear out, he seemed to take my inner organs; and I was left utterly consumed with the love of God. I was also in great pain and it was so severe that I moaned out loud. The pain induced a feeling of joy so intense that I wanted it to last forever.

Teresa of Avila:
Autobiography 29

The soul's dark night

God cures our imperfections by putting the soul into a dark night. Through pure dryness and interior darkness he weans us away from the breast of earthly gratification and delight, and draws us away from all trivial and childish concerns; and he leads us into the path of virtue. Even if we practise every kind of self-mortification with great passion and zeal, we achieve nothing until God purges us by means of the dark night and we passively submit.

This night, which is experienced through contemplation, causes two kinds of darkness, according to the two parts of the soul: sensory and spiritual. In the sensory night the senses are purged, and harmonized with the spirit. In the spiritual night the spirit is purged and denuded, and thence prepared for loving union with God.

The sensory night is common, and happens to many people; those beginning in the way of prayer experience it. The spiritual night is reserved for a few – those who are becoming proficient. The sensory night is bitter and terrible; but is nothing compared with the spiritual night.

John of the Cross: Dark Night of the Soul 1.7, 8

Signs of the dark night

It is easy to confuse the dark night of the soul with the mental disturbance that can be caused by sin, weakness, tepidness of spirit, melancholy, or some bodily illness. There are three principal ways of discerning whether dryness and darkness are caused by these problems, or whether they are truly the means of spiritual cleansing.

The first is that during the dark night the soul derives no satisfaction or consolation from worship, nor from material blessings. God puts the soul into the dark night because he wants the sensory appetites to wither away; so he does not allow the soul to find any sweetness or delight in anything.

The second sign is that during the dark night the soul feels it is no longer serving God, but turning away from him. Normally in times of difficulty the soul turns to God for help; but the soul feels such distaste for God during the dark night, that it cannot ask his aid. It is obvious that this aversion to God is not the result of laxity, but is caused by God himself, taking his strength away from the senses.

The third sign is that during the dark night the soul feels utterly powerless. Its efforts to meditate and to use its imagination in order to sense God's presence, which had previously been effective, now prove useless. God no longer communicates through the senses, as he did before, nor through reflection on the doctrines of the faith. Instead he begins to communicate in a purely spiritual manner, directly with the soul; and the form of communication involves neither the heart nor the mind – neither feelings nor thoughts.

John of the Cross: Dark Night of the Soul 1.10

From darkness to light

During the dark night you should not try to meditate on theological or doctrinal matters, since this is not the appropriate time. You should allow your soul to be quiet and tranquil. You may feel that you are wasting your time, and you may be inclined to rebuke yourself for laxity. But if you remain patient and relaxed, your lack of activity will itself accomplish a great deal.

All that is required is freedom of soul, in which you liberate yourself from the hindrance and weariness of rational thought. You should content yourself with a loving and peaceful attentiveness to God, and be utterly unconcerned that you cannot taste or feel God – nor have any desire to taste or feel him. You should remember that your desires and feelings disturb and distract the soul; so idleness is the appropriate response to the dark night.

Even though the night darkens your spirit, its purpose is to impart light. Even though it humbles you, revealing the depth of your wretchedness, its purpose is to exalt and uplift you. Even though it empties you of all feeling and detaches you from all natural pleasures, its purpose is to fill you with spiritual joy and attach you to the source of that joy.

John of the Cross: Dark Night of the Soul 1.10; 2.9

Ivy on a tree

There are particular acts and movements that a soul can make in prayer, in order to be more closely united and joined to God's goodness. We should make a distinction between uniting and joining. Think of ivy on a tree. The ivy does not simply stand in unity with the tree; it clings to the tree, penetrating the bark, so that it actually joins itself to the trunk. In prayer we not only stand in unity with God, but we also cling to him and penetrate him in love, so we are joined to him.

This happens through small and frequent advances of the soul towards God. If you watch a little infant united and joined to its mother's breast, you will see that from time to time it presses her breast with its face; this movement is stimulated by the pleasure the infant takes in drinking her milk. So too the soul in prayer can press itself more closely to God, stimulated by the pleasure of divine sweetness.

At other times the soul grows closer to God, not through repeated movements, but by continual pressure. Observe a large lump of lead or brass, or a large stone, sitting on the ground. It does not force its way downward; it is gradually pushed by its own weight into the earth. Similarly when the soul rests on God in prayer, its own dependence on God pushes it further and further down into God's love.

Francis de Sales: On the Love of God 7.1

Bees in a hive

Think of a swarm of bees about to take flight. The beekeeper can call the swarm back by softly striking a metal basin, and by filling the air with the aroma of wine mixed with honey; the swarm stops, and goes back into the hive. So too, when we are tempted to flee from him, the Saviour softly utters words of love, and pours the most delicious spiritual wine into our hearts; so we are drawn into the depths of the soul, to enjoy his sweetness.

Wine sweetened with honey is also used to pacify bees. When they start to attack and destroy one another, the best remedy is for the beekeeper to pour honeyed wine amongst them. When the bees smell this pungent and pleasant odour, they become peaceful; they sit quietly, relishing the fragrance. Similarly, when our hearts are in turmoil, God pours his spiritual wine into us – and all the warring powers of the soul fall into a delightful repose. We feel and sense nothing except the fragrance of God's love. We do not even have religious thoughts; we simply enjoy God.

Francis de Sales: On the Love of God 7.2

The clinging child

Consider a child clinging to the breast and neck of its mother. If you want to put the child in its cradle, it resists as best it can, because it prefers the comfort of its mother's bosom. If you force one of its hands to let go, the child grabs with the other. If you lift the child up, it bursts out crying, and looks down with longing eyes to its mother; it does not stop crying until its mother has rocked it to sleep.

In the same way, when the soul has become truly a child of God, it clings to God, and cannot be taken away except by force. If we distract the imagination of such a soul, or if we confuse its intellect, it continues to cling by means of the will. If by some violent disturbance we compel the will to abandon its hold, the soul continues to look at God with deep longing. The soul can never be entirely detached from God; and it will return to God at every opportunity.

Francis de Sales: On the Love of God 7.3

A ball of wax

The devout heart is like a ball of wax in the hands of God, receiving with equal readiness all the impressions that God wishes to make. The devout heart does not want to assert itself, but is entirely passive in the face of God's will; it wants whatever God wants.

In God's eyes various options may be acceptable; the devout heart chooses the best, regardless of cost. God accepts both service to the rich and service to the poor; but since God prefers service to the poor, the devout heart chooses it. God accepts both moderation in pleasure, and patience amid tribulation; but since God prefers the latter, the devout heart prefers it also.

In short, the devout heart regards God's will as its king.

Francis de Sales: On the Love of God 9.6

The original source

God is both my final goal and my original source. If I should find God, I should become what he is; I should shine within his radiance; my words would be within his Word. I should be made divine.

Where is my dwelling place? Where can I never stand by my own strength? Where is my final goal, to which I should ascend? My dwelling place is the place where I cannot stand; it is beyond all place, and above all place.

God loves me above all creatures – just as he loves all creatures above all creatures. I give him as much as I receive from him.

God is far beyond all words that I can express. I cannot speak to him properly in words and he does not speak to me fully in words. I speak to him best, and he speaks to me best, in silence. I hear him and I worship him without words.

It is in my hands to determine whether God blesses me. It is within your hands whether God blesses you. All that is required, is to give consent, and submit.

Angelus Silesius: The Cherubic Wanderer I

The purest nothing

As long as you feel yourself to be a distinct individual, you still carry a burden. As long as you have knowledge, and thus are a subject observing objects, you still carry a burden. As long as you possess material things, you still carry a burden. As long as you cherish objects, and yet are not unified with them, you still carry a burden.

God is the purest nothing. He is untouched by time and space. He does not exist in the realm of human knowledge. The more you reach out for him, the more he escapes your grasp.

To love is very difficult. Yet loving is not enough. We must become love. The subject and the object must become one.

God lives in supreme light. There is no path that gives access to that light. You yourself must become that light; only by becoming supreme light can you see God.

The Spirit of God breathed into us to bring us to life; he is the source of life. He invites us to return to him, and immerse ourselves in him; he wants us constantly to inhale him.

Angelus Silesius: The Cherubic Wanderer I

The soul's element

The bird flies in the air. The stone rests on the earth. The fish swims in the water. The soul's element is the hand of God.

If you graft yourself onto God, you will bear green leaves and exquisite blossom. God's Holy Spirit will be your sap, making the leaves and the flowers grow. Your beauty will be his beauty.

Heaven with its joy lives within you, as does hell with its pain. You may choose whether heaven grows in your soul, or hell – whether you are joyful or miserable.

If I were to despair of ever becoming perfect, I should be denying the power of God. I should also be denying his providence, since he wants to make me perfect.

Go to where you cannot go; there you will meet God. See what you cannot see; you will look on the face of God. Hear what you cannot hear; you will listen to the words of God.

Angelus Silesius: The Cherubic Wanderer I

Knowing nothing

O sweetest revelry! God has become my wine, my meat and my table. And God is my music as I dine.

God is that which he is; I am that which I am. If I were to know myself well, I should know God. If I were to know God well, I should know myself.

If I see Christ in my neighbour, then I both know Christ and know my neighbour. I see the divine light that shines in every person and that light is Christ.

I am God's child; yet he has been born within me. How can both these propositions be true? And yet they are true.

God does not lack worshippers; the natural sound of every creature is a hymn of praise. The sounds of nature are in perfect harmony; let human voices join the chorus.

When you now God, you know nothing. Those who know him, must become one with him; and in him there is no subject and object, no knower and knowledge.

Angelus Silesius: The Cherubic Wanderer 1

Divine harmony

The will of God is the essence and power of all things; and the will of God harmonizes all things with the soul. Without the will of God all is nothingness and emptiness, lies and vanity, the letter without the spirit, husks without kernels, death. The will of God is salvation and health, life to the body and soul.

The will of God within an object cannot be perceived merely by looking at the object's external appearance; nor can it be perceived by assessing whether the object may be helpful to your body or soul, because that in itself is utterly unimportant. The will of God is the process by which any object or event forms the image of Jesus Christ in your heart. You should not desire one object or event rather than another, because God can bring all things into unity with you.

Sometimes pleasant ideas fill the mind; sometimes the mind is distracted and confused. Sometimes pleasant emotions fill the heart; sometimes the heart is disturbed and anxious. Sometimes the body is well, and sometimes it is sick. Yet in every situation and in every moment the divine will is active, loving you and sustaining you. Without the divine will, bread would be poison; with it, poison can become nourishment. Without the divine will, books would darken the mind; with it, darkness would become light. The divine will makes all things good and true; and thus all things become blessings from God.

Jean-Pierre de Caussade:
Self-abandonment to Divine Providence 1

Divine fullness

The soul that is not attracted to the will of God, will find neither contentment nor sanctification in acts of worship or in acts of charity. If you are not satisfied by what God chooses for you, then nothing will satisfy you. If you are disgusted with the food that God has provided for you, then every other food will seem even more insipid. A soul can only be truly nourished, strengthened, purified, enriched and sanctified by the divine fullness of the present moment. What more do you want? Since all good is contained in the present moment, why look elsewhere? Do you know better than God? If he has ordained a particular event, why desire a different event?

Can the wisdom and goodness of God be wrong? Do you think you will find peace by struggling against his might? Is not resistance to God – which we often make, but rarely admit – the cause of our inner disturbance and discontent?

The soul that refuses to be satisfied by the divine fullness of the present moment, will be punished by being unable to find satisfaction elsewhere. The soul that accepts God's design as it is, and embraces the present moment, finds serenity and peace.

Jean-Pierre de Caussade:
Self-abandonment to Divine Providence 1

Divine design

Once the soul perceives that all things are fashioned by God, the soul derives spiritual value from all things. Every object, and all that is contained in every object, becomes holy and perfect; everything that the soul sees, becomes perfect in its sight.

But in order not to stray from the right path, the soul must be careful. It must not follow every inspiration; it should first ensure that the inspiration truly comes from God. The test is whether the inspiration enables the soul to grow in holiness; and holiness consists in submitting to the designs of God.

Nothing must be rejected which God offers; nothing should be sought which is not offered by God. The purpose of spiritual reading, of listening to the teaching and advice of the wise, of public worship, and of quiet meditation, is to instruct you in the ways of God, and to unite your designs to his.

Jean-Pierre de Caussade:
Self-abandonment to Divine Providence 1

Divine workings

All creatures live in the hands of God. The senses perceive only outward action; but faith perceives the actions of God in every event. Faith knows that Jesus Christ is alive in all things, and operates through the course of history – century by century. Faith knows that the briefest moment and the tiniest atom contain a portion of Christ's hidden life and his mysterious power. Outward activity is a veil concealing the inner workings of God.

Most of us do not possess faith that is sufficiently pure or penetrating to see this clearly; but sometimes God takes us by surprise, drawing back the veil in order to deepen our faith.

Jean-Pierre de Caussade:
Self-abandonment to Divine Providence 2

The treasure of the present moment

If you are able to respond to each moment as a manifestation of God's will, you will find in each moment everything that the heart can desire. What can be more reasonable and more perfect than God's will? Its infinite value could not be increased by some change in time, place and circumstance.

If you have discovered the secret of finding God's will at every moment and in every event, you possess the most precious gift on earth. You do not need to desire anything else. You do not need to hanker after more wealth. Everything you truly want at any moment, is contained in the events of that moment.

The present moment is always full of infinite treasure. It contains far more than you can possibly grasp. Faith is the measure of its riches: what you find in the present moment is according to the measure of your faith. Love also is the measure: the more the heart loves, the more it rejoices in what God provides. The will of God presents itself at each moment like an immense ocean that the desire of your heart cannot empty; yet you will drink from that ocean according to your faith and love.

Jean-Pierre de Caussade:
Self-abandonment to Divine Providence 3

Concepts and experience

Religion can be grasped without reason, otherwise no one could possess religion except those with intelligence. Moreover, if religion depended on reason, theologians would always excel in holiness; experience tells us this is not so.

The truth of concepts matters far less than the truth of experience. Errors of doctrine matter far less than errors of the heart. An ignorant person is far less evil than a stubborn person.

Understanding reached from concepts changes with time, education and other circumstances. Understanding reached from experience is not subject to these changes; it simply deepens with time and circumstances.

The experience central to religion is receiving God's revelation of himself. That which God does not want human beings to understand, he does not reveal. That which he does want human beings to understand, he does reveal. It may sometimes be useful to express divine revelations in concepts; it is never necessary.

Nikolaus von Zinzendorf: The German Socrates

Faith in distress

We cannot create faith within ourselves. God must work within us, giving us new birth, so that the heart, spirit, mind and all the faculties are transformed. This transformation is the essence of faith. And if faith is to enter us, it must be preceded by distress, which opens our ears to it.

This distress comes when we recognize ourselves to be spiritually poor, when we see that we have no saviour, and when we become palpably aware of our own misery. We see our own corruption, and become profoundly anxious because of it. We desperately look out for someone to help us, and are willing to accept the first offer of aid without examination or investigation.

What results from this faith, which arises out of a desire for salvation? Thankful love results from it. An unknown man appears. Yet even though we do not know him, the heart says: 'He wants to help, he wants to give comfort; and he can help and give comfort. He is the one I heard about in my youth. They call him the saviour, the Son of God, the Lord Jesus. He must help me. If only he would come to my aid! If only he would take my soul into his care, so that it would not perish! Lord, have mercy!'

Nikolaus von Zinzendorf: *Saving Faith*

Implicit and explicit faith

Faith arising from distress may be called implicit faith; it operates within the heart alone, and is not visible to anyone else. It must then lead to explicit faith, which unfolds and manifests itself to others.

Explicit faith has two parts. The first part consists in learning. We want to find out about our saviour. We want to know him from head to foot, in heart and body. We want to penetrate his nature, both as he is now, and as he was on earth in the flesh. We think deeply about him and his teaching; we instruct ourselves about the truths he taught, one after the other, using both the faculty of reason to understand them in the mind, and the faculty of emotion to grasp them in the heart. We go and speak to those who know and love the saviour.

Thus, we find ourselves falling in love with our saviour, rejoicing in the happiness with which he fills the heart. We take pleasure in meditating on him; and our joy is enhanced when through him we encounter the Father and the Holy Spirit.

Now comes the second part of explicit faith. Having learned about our faith, we now want to tell others about it. We want to proclaim the wounds of Christ, from which God's power flows; we want to proclaim his wounded heart, from which God's love flows. And our faith is so vibrant that we are able to speak with conviction and assurance. Our faith flows out of us with divine power and love, pouring itself at the feet of all we meet.

Nikolaus von Zinzendorf: Saving Faith

PERSONAL TESTIMONY

Although Christians had written in personal terms in earlier centuries, the Protestant Reformation, by emphasizing the importance of individual experience, encouraged people to recount in intimate detail their spiritual story.

George Fox (d. 1691), who founded the Quakers, kept a Journal, as did John Wesley (d. 1791), who founded the Methodists; their accounts of their conversions typify Protestant spirituality.

Jonathan Edwards (d. 1758) and David Brainerd (d. 1747) described their efforts as missionaries, one in an American colonial town, and the other amongst native Americans. John Woolman (d. 1772) in his Journal related in poignant detail his attempts, inspired by his faith, to speak out against slavery.

Leo Tolstoy (d. 1910), the great Russian novelist, rejected the complacent Christianity of his childhood, and strove to follow Christ's moral teaching to the letter. Charles Haddon Spurgeon (d. 1892), a great preacher, claimed to have visits at night from Christ himself.

Amongst Roman Catholics the most popular personal testimony is that of Thérèse of Lisieux, a French nun who died in her mid-twenties.

The voice of Christ

I fasted frequently, and walked from place to place alone. I often sat under a tree, and studied my Bible until the sun set. Then I walked through the night, filled with sadness and self-pity. I was truly a man of sorrows.

I had no respect for priests, and for a time I sought guidance from independent ministers. They usually treated me warmly, but I soon despaired of them; none could speak to my condition. When I realized that no human being on earth could help me, nor even tell me how I could find help, I heard a voice which said: 'There is one, Christ Jesus, who can speak to your condition.' And when I heard this voice in my heart, I leapt for joy.

Then the Lord showed me why no one on earth could speak to my condition – namely, that I should give all the glory to him. All people are imprisoned by sin and ignorance, as I had been, in order that Jesus might save them. When God is at work, who can hinder him? For me, faith was now a matter of experience.

To my eyes all things now seemed new. Creation now had a new fragrance, so sweet that it cannot be described in words. I knew nothing but purity, innocence and goodness. I had been renewed in the image of God, by the power of Jesus Christ.

George Fox: Journal 1647, 1648

The inner light

I saw that Christ had died for all people, and was a propiti-
ation for all people. I saw that he had enlightened all men
and women with his divine and saving light, and that only
those believing in this light are true believers. I saw that
the grace of God, which brings salvation, has appeared to all
people, and that the Spirit of God has also been given to all
people for their benefit.

These things I did not see with the help of other human
beings, nor by reading them in a book. I saw them by the
light of Jesus Christ, and by his Spirit – just as the writers of
the scriptures saw them. Despite having this direct knowledge, I still greatly respect the scriptures, which are very precious to me; indeed I value them precisely because they were
written by the same light that illuminates my life.

George Fox: Journal 1648

Against church buildings

As I approached Nottingham, I came to the top of a hill. I looked down on the city, and saw in the middle a vast church with a high steeple. It struck me with great force that people worship the building and its steeple, in place of God; the building is an idol.

I heard within me the voice of the Lord, saying: 'Go into the city, and with a loud voice condemn that building and those who worship in it.' When I entered the church, the people within it seemed to me like fallow ground, and the priest in the pulpit was like a great lump of earth. The Lord's power came upon me with such force that I could not hold myself back. I told them that God does not live in temples made with human hands, and that they must allow the Holy Spirit to enter their souls – the Spirit that alone can lead them to the truth.

As I spoke, police officers came, and took me away. They hurled me into a stinking prison.

George Fox: Journal 1649

Response to violence

After I had entered the church in Ulverston, and spoken against idolatry, some members of the congregation rushed towards me, and attacked me with their fists and with books; and when they had pushed me to the ground, they trampled on me. Other people, including the priests, ran out of the church, for fear of being hurt themselves in the violence. Then an officer cried out: 'Give him to me!' He pushed his way through the crowd, grabbed me, and led me out of the church. He handed me over to four constables, and ordered them to take me out of the town and whip me.

They dragged me along a muddy lane. People friendly to me followed, and the constables hit them over the heads with truncheons; I saw blood running down many faces. A loyal supporter ran after me, but the constables threw him into a ditch – and they threatened to knock all the teeth out of his head.

Finally they took me into a field, and whipped me with rods made from willow. Many of those who had attacked me in the church had gathered round; and, after whipping me, the constables handed me over to them. They hit me with their walking sticks on the head, arms and shoulders, until I was unconscious.

When my consciousness returned, the power of the Lord surged through me. I stretched out my arms, and exclaimed: 'Strike me again.' A man came forward, and struck my hands so hard that they bled. I looked upon the wounds with love; and then I looked on my persecutors with love.

George Fox: Journal 1652

A good soldier

After a while the power of the Lord surged through me again. My hands stopped bleeding and the pain went; and I felt better than I had ever felt before. My enemies were so startled by my recovery that they backed away; and they started arguing amongst themselves.

Then a group came forward, and said that, if I gave them money, they would protect me from further attacks. I refused their offer, and was moved by the Lord to speak to them about spiritual matters. I told them that human beings have no need of priests, because every human being can have direct communication with God. They became angry, and declared that, if I ever came to their town again, they would kill me.

I was immediately moved by the Lord to defy them. I went back into Ulverston market-place, where I met a soldier carrying a sword. 'Sir,' he said to me, 'I am your servant. I am ashamed you have been abused, because you are a fine and righteous man.' He promised to assist me as best he could. I told him that I was not frightened, because the Lord's power is greater than any human power.

As I walked around the market, the soldier followed me, pointing his sword towards the crowd. I begged him to put his sword away, and he did so. Yet despite being unarmed, no one attacked us.

George Fox: Journal 1652

Childhood obedience

I believe that, until I was about ten years old, I had not sinned against that washing by the Holy Spirit that was given to me in baptism. I had been very strictly educated and I had been taught that I could only be saved by obeying all the commandments of God. Indeed, I was told precisely how each commandment should be obeyed. I gladly accepted all these instructions; and, as far as outward duties and sins are concerned, this ensured that I was faultless. But whatever was said to me about inner obedience and holiness, I neither understood nor remembered. As a result I was as ignorant of the true meaning of the divine law as I was of the gospel of Christ.

The next six or seven years were spent at school. Outward restrictions were now removed, and my behaviour worsened. I neglected many of my duties and I was frequently guilty of some outward sin; but my sins were not so bad as to cause scandal in the eyes of the world.

However, I still read the scriptures, and I said my prayers every morning and evening. And I now hoped to be saved by not being as bad as other people, and by religious observance. And when I went to university for five years, I continued to pray both in public and in private, and I read numerous religious books, especially commentaries on the scriptures.

Yet I still had no notion of inner holiness. And my only inner activity consisted of occasional fits of repentance.

John Wesley: Journal

Youthful good works

In 1730 I began visiting prisons, assisting the poor and the sick in town, and doing what other good my abilities and my limited funds could accomplish. To increase the money I had available to give away, I eliminated all luxuries from my life, as well as much that people would call necessary. I soon became renowned for my frugality, and I took pleasure in this reputation.

The following spring I started to observe the Wednesday and Friday fasts, which were commonly practised in the early church, eating nothing until three in the afternoon. I wondered what other religious observance I could adopt, but could think of nothing. I watched over myself constantly to ensure I committed no sin, and I took every opportunity for doing good.

I knew that all this was worthless unless it were directed towards inner holiness. I had in my mind an image of God, and I thought of myself as submitting my will to his. Yet, after living in this manner for some years, I had a serious illness that brought me close to death; and I felt no assurance that God had accepted me. This shocked me, because I did not realize that I had been building on sand.

John Wesley: Journal

Adult ignorance

In January 1738 I was again in imminent danger of death. Inwardly I felt very uneasy and fearful; and I was convinced that the cause of my fear was my unbelief. Thus I was determined to acquire a true and living faith. Yet still I did not truly understand the right object of faith; I meant only faith in God, and not faith in and through Jesus Christ. In my ignorance I did not realize that I was completely empty of this faith; I simply thought I did not have enough of it.

I came to London, and met a man called Peter Boehler – a meeting that God had planned. Peter Boehler said to me that a true faith in Christ invariably has two fruits: dominion over sin, and a constant peace deriving from a sense of forgiveness. I was amazed at this notion, as if it were some new gospel. I said to myself that, if this man was right, I clearly lacked all faith. But I was not willing to admit this. So I argued with him, and tried to prove that faith can exist without these fruits.

John Wesley: Journal

Final conversion

That evening I went very unwillingly to a meeting in Aldersgate Street, where someone read Luther's *Preface to the Letter to the Romans*. At about a quarter to nine, while he was describing the change that God makes in the heart through faith in Christ, I felt my heart strangely warmed. I felt I trusted Christ, and Christ alone, for my salvation; and an assurance was given to me that he had taken away my sins, and saved me from death.

I began to pray with all my might for those who in some particular way had abused me or persecuted me. I then testified openly to all present what I now felt in my heart. But it was not long before the thought came into my head: 'This cannot be faith. Where is your joy?' Then I remembered what I had been taught: that peace and victory over sin are essential to faith in Christ, but that God gives and withholds joy as he chooses, according to his own will.

When I returned home, I was greatly buffeted by temptations; but I cried out to God and they fled away. They returned again and again; and, as they returned, I lifted up my eyes and again cried out to God. In this way I realized the essential difference between my present and my former states. Formerly I was fighting against sin with my own strength; sometimes I won, and sometimes I was defeated. But now Christ was fighting on my behalf, and so I was always the conqueror.

John Wesley: Journal

A young woman's conversion

It was in the latter part of December 1735 that the Spirit of God began to work among us, in a most extraordinary and wonderful way. Suddenly, one after the other, six people were converted, some in a most remarkable manner.

I was particularly surprised by the conversion of a young woman who had been one of the most sociable and gregarious people in the whole town. When she came to see me, I assumed that she was foolish and empty-headed. Yet she told me of how God's power and grace had transformed her: that he had given her a new heart, which was truly submissive and holy. At the time I was convinced she was speaking the truth; and my subsequent observation of her behaviour confirmed this.

Though her transformation was glorious, I was anxious about the effect it might have on others; I feared that some might be hardened by it. But in fact the effect was the opposite, to a wonderful degree. God used it to achieve the greatest spiritual awakening that this town has ever seen.

The news went round the town like a flash of lightning, and seemed to illuminate the hearts of all the young people, as well as many others. Those whose lives were the most frivolous and self-indulgent, whom I most feared would be hardened by her example, were the most affected by it. Soon throughout the town people of all classes and ages were discussing religion; there was hardly a single person who remained indifferent.

Jonathan Edwards: The Great Awakening

A town's awakening

Each day for many months there were instances of sinners being brought out of the darkness into the marvellous light of Christ, with a song of praise for God on their lips. Thus the number of saints in the town rapidly multiplied. By the spring and summer of 1736 the town seemed full of the presence of God; it had never before been so full of love and joy – as well as so full of spiritual anguish amongst those who remained unconverted.

In almost every house there were remarkable signs of God's presence. Parents loved their children as if the children had just been born. Husbands loved their wives, and wives their husbands, as if they had just been wed.

This joy and love was especially manifest in church on Sundays. The public worship was a delight, with a wonderful sense of mutual friendship infusing the congregation. Indeed, the whole congregation seemed to come alive. People prayed with great intensity, and each person was eager to hear the words of the preacher; frequently people wept during the sermons, with sorrow or joy according to what was being said. The hymns were sung with both fervour and skill, the women singing the melodies, and the men singing the other three parts. Even weddings, which previously had been rather frivolous occasions, were now filled with spiritual joy.

There was a further consequence of this awakening: people who had already been believers were now renewed in their faith; and all doubts, which may have crept into their souls, were dispelled.

Jonathan Edwards: *The Great Awakening*

A comfortless mission

Wednesday, March 9, 1743 – Rode sixteen miles to Montauk. I enjoyed some inward sweetness on the road; but, when I arrived and saw the Indians, I felt flat and depressed. I went off alone and tried to pray, but felt horribly abandoned by God. I then preached, and received some assistance from the Spirit, and I trust I conveyed something of God's presence in our midst. In the evening I prayed again, and gave personal encouragement to some of the people. May the God of all grace enable my labours to succeed in this place.

Friday, April 1 – I rode to Kaunaumeek, near twenty miles from Stockbridge, where another group of Indians live. I slept the night on a little heap of straw.

Lord's Day, April 10 – Rose early in the morning, and walked out into the woods, where I spent a considerable time in prayer and meditation. I preached to the Indians, both in the morning and the afternoon. In general they behaved in a sober manner. Two or three seemed to show some particular interest in my words, and I spoke to them privately afterwards. One of them told me that her heart had cried ever since she had first heard me speak.

Wednesday, May 18 – My circumstances are such that I have no external comforts of any kind; I have only the inner comforts that God provides. I live in a wilderness, with only one person, my Indian interpreter, with whom I can converse in English. My diet consists mostly of boiled corn, and I sleep on straw. But the Indians themselves have an even harder life.

David Brainerd: Diary

An eloquent sermon

August 8 – This afternoon I preached to about thirty-five Indians, men, women and children. I felt unusually eloquent, with the right words coming easily to me. As I spoke many of them seemed to become agitated. Afterwards, when I spoke to many of them privately, the power of God seemed to descend like a great wind, with energy that no one could resist.

I was amazed at the effect on the people. Old men and women, who had been drunken wretches for many years, were suddenly concerned about their souls; so were many small children, some only six or seven years old. Even middle-aged men with stubborn hearts were visibly moved. One of the leading Indian men had told me the previous night that he became a Christian ten years ago and now he was bitterly repentant that he had not lived in accordance with his faith. Another man, who had been a murderer and a notorious drunkard, was also induced to beg God for mercy, weeping profusely as he did so.

A young Indian woman, who had not realized that she had a soul, and who had previously mocked me, said to me that she could now feel the soul within her. She seemed as if she had been pierced by a dart; she clutched her chest, and cried out repeatedly, 'Lord, have mercy on me!'

David Brainerd: Diary

Visions of God's love

Although my parents were humble labourers, I learnt as a child to read and write; and in my teenage years I spent winter evenings and other leisure times reading books, in order to improve my education.

When I was aged twenty-one, I met a man who owned a bakery and a shop; and he asked me to work for him, tending the shop and keeping the accounts. I told my father about this proposal and, after some deliberation, he allowed me to accept. After a while I stopped meeting with my old friends, as I found their company crude, and I started to mix with people whose conversation was helpful to me.

At the age of twenty-three I had many visions, revealing to me the love which God has for all his creatures, and for human beings in particular as the most noble of them. Soon after these visions my employer, who had a black female slave, decided to sell her; and he ordered me to write the bill of sale. The command was unexpected and, although I felt uneasy about colluding with slavery, I felt compelled to obey it. But afterwards my conscience was greatly troubled and I said, both to my employer and to the man who bought the woman, that slavery is wrong.

John Woolman: Journal

Speaking out

Many good people in my church kept slaves but, despite their goodness, I became more and more convinced of the evil of slavery. On one occasion a fellow-member, who had recently purchased a slave, asked me to write a conveyance for him. I told him that I was unwilling to write it; and, in a gentle and courteous tone, I explained my views. He replied that he too was uneasy about slavery; but since his wife wanted a slave, he felt he had no choice but to provide her with one.

In 1753 a man came to see me, whose brother was sick; the man asked me to write his brother's will. He told me that his brother owned slaves, and wished to leave them to his children. Since writing wills is highly profitable, and since I dislike offending people, I was inclined to fulfil the man's request. But then I looked to God, and felt guided to speak out. I told the man that keeping slaves is wrong; and I said that I was unable to collude with it by writing the will. He replied that many good Christians keep slaves. But I was adamant.

John Woolman: Journal

A shifting argument

Five years later, when I was on a journey, I met a colonel in the militia, who seemed a thoughtful man. In the course of conversation I made a distinction between those who work for their living, and are frugal in their habits, and those who live on the labour of slaves; and I said that the former are happier than the latter. The colonel agreed, but then spoke of the laziness of Negroes; he said that one white worker does as much in a day as a black slave does in two or three days. I said that the difference between them lies not in the colour of their skins, but in their status: a free man knows that the fruits of his work will benefit his own family, while a slave knows that only his owner benefits – so he has no incentive to work hard.

The colonel was not persuaded by this argument. So I shifted my ground to the issue of power, saying that when people have power over others, they usually abuse it; thus the owners of slaves are liable to treat them badly. I concluded that liberty and equality are the natural rights of all human beings. The colonel did not deny this, but he too shifted his ground, saying that the lives of the Negroes in Africa is so wretched, that they are better off being shipped here as slaves. I replied that we should act according to principle, not according to some doubtful calculation of benefits. And there our conversation ended.

John Woolman: Journal

Loving enemies

When I understood that the words 'love your enemies' actually mean what they say, my whole understanding of Christ's teaching suddenly changed. I was appalled at the peculiar way I had understood it until then. I knew – we all know – that the centre of Christ's teaching lies in love for other people. But I now realized the essence of love: you should love those who hate and despise you.

Since childhood I had frequently heard Christ's command to 'turn the other cheek' when someone strikes you; and the command to 'love your enemies' was equally familiar. But why had I not understood these simple words in a simple manner? Why had I searched instead for some allegorical meaning in them?

Their meaning is indeed simple. If someone is violent towards you, then you are not violent in return. If someone insults you, then you do not respond with an insult. If the person, Jesus Christ, giving these commands is divine, how can I say that I lack the strength to obey them? If a master commands a young and healthy labourer to chop wood, the labourer does not reply that he lacks the strength to do so.

Leo Tolstoy: What I Believe

Contradicting Christ

Throughout my childhood I was taught that Christ is divine, so his teaching is infallible. But I was also taught to respect those institutions that used violence in order to protect me from evil people. I had even been taught to regard these institutions as holy. I was taught that it is shameful and degrading to submit to those who do evil, and that it is praiseworthy to resist them.

As I grew up, I was taught to judge those younger than me, and to punish them when they did wrong. And then, as a young man, I was taught to be a soldier; I was shown how to murder those who do evil. The army, of which I was a member, was called a Christian army; and Christian priests blessed its weapons and its actions.

In short, from childhood to adulthood I was taught to behave in a manner that directly contradicts the commands of Christ: to fight against those who do evil and to take revenge on those who injure or insult me, my family or my nation. And I was taught that this behaviour is actually Christian.

Everything around me – my safety, my security, my family, and my property – was based on a law that Christ had specifically repudiated, the law of a tooth for a tooth.

Leo Tolstoy: What I Believe

Word and deed

At various points in my childhood I questioned the contradiction between Christ's teaching and normal behaviour. Church teachers told me that human frailty made Christ's teaching impossible to obey – and that Christ would therefore excuse us. Thus church leaders were in effect admitting what the secular opponents of Christianity constantly assert: that Christ's teaching is utterly impractical, and is a mere fantasy. This admission of the impracticality of Christianity was instilled into me so consistently, that it came to seem quite reasonable; moreover it was entirely in tune with my own desires. So by adulthood the contradiction had ceased to trouble me.

I did not see that it is impossible to profess Christ, the basis of whose teaching is loving your enemies, and at the same time strive calmly and deliberately to uphold the law courts, the government, the army – all of which exist to destroy those who are seen as enemies. I did not see that it is impossible to follow a way of life that is contrary to Christ's teaching, and at the same time to pray to Christ for his kingdom on earth.

My error consisted in accepting Christ in word, but denying him in deed.

Leo Tolstoy: What I Believe

An engine without transmission

The commandment to love your enemies unifies the whole teaching of Christ – if it is seen as obligatory on everyone, and not a mere saying.

It is the key that opens everything, but only if it is pushed into the lock. To regard this commandment as a mere saying, which cannot be followed without supernatural help, is to destroy the whole of Christ's teaching. And a teaching from which the basic unifying commandment has been removed, inevitably appears impossible in all its aspects. To unbelievers it seems simply ridiculous – and it cannot appear otherwise.

It is as if we had installed an engine, heated up the boiler, set it in motion, but not attached the transmission belt. That is what we have done by saying that it is possible to be a

Christian without fulfilling the commandment to love your enemies.

Leo Tolstoy: What I Believe

Common humanity

There is a constant temptation to regard one's own nation as superior to other nations, and to regard other nations as potential enemies. Indeed, in absent-minded moments feelings of superiority and enmity towards people of other nations continue to arise within me. I must immediately acknowledge these feelings to be false. I must never allow myself to start justifying them, enumerating in my mind the errors, cruelties and barbarities of other nations. On the contrary, I must commit myself anew to be as friendly towards foreigners as I am towards my compatriots.

The source of the temptation is the delusion that my own welfare is bound up only with the people of my own nation, and not with all the other people on this earth. In truth my unity with all people cannot be severed by frontiers of government decrees. I know that all people everywhere are my brothers and sisters. The enmity between nations has caused untold evil and suffering; and I must expose patriotism, which puts love of country above love of humanity, as a monstrous fraud.

We are all children of one loving Father.

Leo Tolstoy: What I Believe

A first visit from the Lord

I remember well when God first visited me and I was affected in the same way as Saul of Tarsus was affected when the Lord spoke to him out of heaven. God brought me down from my high horse, and hurled me down on the ground. By the brightness of his Holy Spirit he made me blind; and, in my desperation, I cried to God for help and guidance.

I felt that I had been rebelling against the Lord, taking opportunities to do evil as they arose, and my soul was filled with anguish at this realization. Jesus seemed to stare at me and his eye penetrated me, revealing the depth of my sin; and this caused me to go outside and weep bitterly. I was stripped of all pretence of righteousness and stood naked before the Lord. And then the Lord clothed me with songs of praise.

Although it was night, I was not dreaming. On the contrary, then and there I ceased dreaming, and began to grapple with the inner reality of my life.

Having clothed me, the Lord then showed me the injuries he had sustained on the cross, when nails had been driven into his flesh; and I knew that I had wielded the hammer. This knowledge made my anguish almost too much to bear. I begged for forgiveness – and he responded by softening my heart.

Charles Haddon Spurgeon: An Address

Later visits from the Lord

Since that time I have had many visits from the Lord; and, while the first visit was sharply searching, the later visits have given me comfort and solace.

These visits have come when I have found myself unable to sleep. The night is still, everybody is quiet, there is no work to be done – and then the Lord draws near. Sometimes this happens when I am suffering some physical pain, such as a headache or a throbbing heart; but as soon as Jesus comes, my bed of suffering becomes a throne of glory.

It is true that God gives us sleep. But at these times he gives something far better than sleep – his own presence, and the fullness of joy that comes with it.

Do you ask me to describe these manifestations of the Lord? It is hard to tell you in words; you must know them for yourselves. If you had never tasted sweetness, no one could describe the sensation of eating honey; you can only taste and see. To a person born blind, sight must be beyond imagination; and to someone who has not been visited by the Lord, his visits are far beyond conception.

Each of us is assured of salvation; but a visit from the Lord is more than this. To know that Jesus loves me, is one thing; to be visited by him in love is quite another.

Charles Haddon Spurgeon: An Address

The effects of visits

What have been the effects on me of the Lord's visits? I may describe them simply: peace, then rest, and then spiritual joy. I am not speaking of some emotional excitement, arising from fanatical rapture; I speak of the experience of the Lord's great heart touching mine, and my heart rising in sympathy.

As I say, the first effect is peace. Within the soul all war is over, and a blessed peace is proclaimed – the peace of God that passes all understanding.

The second effect is rest. All personal ambitions fade away, and all desires disappear. I am enveloped by a divine serenity and security. I have no thought of enemies; I have no fears or doubts. I joyfully lay aside my own will. I am nothing, and I shall be nothing; Christ is everything, and his will is the pulse of my soul. I am perfectly content to be either ill or well, to be either rich or poor, to be slandered or honoured; I merely want to abide in the love of Christ. Jesus fills the horizon of my being.

And the third effect is joy; a flood of joy fills my mind. I half wish that dawn may never come, for fear that its light will banish the superior light of Christ's presence. I wish my beloved Lord would take me away with him. I long to hear the voices of his white-robed soldiers, who follow their divine leader wherever he goes.

There is a lasting effect. Through these visits I am persuaded there is no great distance between earth and heaven; the distance exists only in our dull minds.

Charles Haddon Spurgeon: An Address

Wishing to be a saint

I have always wished to be a saint. But whenever I used to compare myself with saints, I was aware of the sad difference: they were like high mountains, their heads shrouded by clouds; while I was only an insignificant grain of sand, lying beneath people's feet.

Yet I refused to be discouraged. I said to myself: 'God would not put ambitions into people's heads that could not be accomplished. Clearly I can never be a great or important person. So it must be possible to become saintly in a very small and insignificant fashion. I shall accept myself as I am, with all my limitations; and then I shall find a little way, all of my own, which will be a shortcut to heaven.'

I continued my musings: 'We live in an age of inventions. Nowadays rich people do not even climb stairs, but go by elevator instead. I am not big enough to climb the steep stairway to perfection. Is there not an elevator that will take me up to Jesus?'

Thérèse of Lisieux: Autobiography 31

Misunderstood intentions

Sometimes an action that seems wrong, is in fact praise-worthy; it depends on the intention. I learned this through a trivial incident; and it taught me that you should never pass judgement on others.

The doorbell had been rung twice, indicating that work-men had arrived bringing some trees for the Christmas crèche. I was bored by the needlework I was doing, and thought I should enjoy lending a hand. The Mother Sub-Prioress spoke to me and the sister sitting beside me, saying that one of us should go and help the workmen. I started to fold up my needlework. But then I thought that the sister be-side me might get particular pleasure from helping the work-men. So I folded my needlework slowly, to let her finish first. The Mother Sub-Prioress was looking with a smile, and said to me: 'Just like you – slow and lazy. There are no extra jewels for your crown today.' And, of course, everyone else must silently have agreed with her.

I cannot tell you how much good this incident did to me. It made me much kinder about other people's faults. And it pricked my vanity. When people speak well of me, I say to myself: 'My efforts to do good are often marked down as faults. So the actions that are marked well may really be faults.'

Thérèse of Lisieux: Autobiography 34

Dealing with irritation

There is one sister in the community who constantly irritated me. Her mannerisms, her way of speaking and her whole character repelled me. But I recognized that she is very holy, so God loves her dearly.

I strived to suppress my feelings towards her. I reminded myself that love is not a matter of pleasant emotions, but of good actions. Thus I decided to behave as if she were the most lovable person I knew. Every time I encountered her, I prayed for her, commending her to God for all her virtues. I felt certain that Jesus would like my prayers, because all artists like to hear their work praised. But I did not confine myself to praying; I also took every opportunity to be kind to her. And when I felt tempted to put her down with an unkind remark, I smiled at her and changed the subject.

She was utterly unaware of my true emotions, so she never realized why I acted in this way. To this day she believes that her personality attracts me. Once at recreation she came over to me, with a broad smile, and said: 'I wish you would tell me why you are especially fond of me; whenever you see me, you give me a sweet look.' In truth I had become fond of her by that time, because I had learned to see Jesus in the depths of her soul.

Thérèse of Lisieux: Autobiography 34

Depending on prayer

I depend completely on prayer. It is my only source of strength; it is the irresistible weapon that our Lord has put into my head. Again and again I have observed my prayers touching people's hearts – far more effectively than any words I could say directly to them. The power of prayer is astonishing. Like a queen, prayer always has access to the King, and can obtain whatever it asks. It is a great mistake to think that prayers can only work if they are taken from a book. If that were true, I should be in a terrible position. I can never face the strain of searching through books of prayers, looking for the one designed to meet my present need – it makes my head spin.

I just do what children have to do before they learn to read. I tell God in my own words what I want, without any splendid turn of phrase, and somehow he always manages to understand me. For me prayer is like a ship being launched into the sea; in prayer I am carried towards God.

Thérèse of Lisieux: Autobiography 37

BIBLIOGRAPHY

There are a number of translations of the works represented in the present volume. These are the most accessible.

Barrois, Georges, ed., *The Fathers Speak* (New York, St. Vladimir's Seminary Press, 1986).

Bettenson, Henry, tr., *The Early Christian Fathers* (London and New York, OUP, 1957).

Bettenson, Henry, tr., *The Later Christian Fathers* (London and New York, OUP, 1970).

Egan, Harvey D., ed., *An Anthology of Christian Mysticism* (Minnesota, The Liturgical Press, 1991).

Jaegher, Paul de, ed., *An Anthology of Mysticism* (London, Burns & Oates, 1935).

Kenneth, Brother, ed., *From the Fathers to the Churches* (London and San Francisco, Collins, 1983).

Staniforth, Maxwell, tr., *Early Christian Writings* (London and New York, Penguin, 1968).

Stevenson, Herbert F., ed., *Light Upon the World: An Anthology of Evangelical Spiritual Writings* (London, Mowbrays, 1979).

Van de Weyer, Robert, ed., *The Illustrated Book of Christian Literature* (Berkhamsted, Arthur James, 1998).

Wirt, Sherwood Eliot, ed., *Spiritual Awakening: Classic Writings of Eighteenth Century Devotion* (Westchester and London, Crossway Books, 1986).

Wirt, Sherwood Eliot, ed., *Spiritual Power: Classic Writings of Nineteenth Century Spirituality* (Westchester and London, Crossway Books, 1989).

The illustrations in this volume have been taken from Farrar, Frederic W., *The Life of Christ as Represented in Art* (London, Adam and Charles Back, 1894).

INDEX OF WRITERS